ORGANIC
GARDENING®

Country
Calendar
&
Planning
Guide

1999

Heidi Stonehill

Vice President and Editorial Director: Margaret J. Lydic
Managing Editor, Rodale Garden Books: Ellen Phillips
Copy Editor: Alison Stubits Ackerman
Editorial assistance: Liz Leone

Cover design: Carol Angstadt
Interior layout: Jerry O'Brien
Interior design coordination: Marta Strait
Cover and interior illustrations: Frank Fretz

Astronomical data compiled with the help of David L. Stonehill

NOTE: Phenomena of the sun, earth, and moon were determined in Eastern
Standard Time or Eastern Daylight Time when appropriate.

INTRODUCTION

Do you remember what made you become a gardener? Sometimes, it's as simple as seeing a beautiful garden on a trip or in a magazine. Perhaps a friend or relative was the inspiration. For me, it was my grandparents who introduced me to gardening and who also played a large part in developing my appreciation for nature. Gramp would often have a vegetable garden in full swing at the Maine cottage where my family vacationed. Nana planted flowers around their permanent home in Massachusetts and later tried her hand at growing herbs. She was also a whiz in the kitchen—making wonderful wholesome meals with the garden harvest and canning and freezing produce left and right. (I don't know where she got the energy!)

Nana loved birds, too. She would put out birdseed every day and especially enjoyed the chickadees and pheasants that came to feed in the wintertime. In summer, I remember helping to fill the stone bird bath with cool water every morning using a tea kettle. It took two or three trips, but it was worth it. Soon after I filled the bird bath and went back inside, I would watch as a few birds would timidly perch on the rim, and then one would be bold enough to plunk right into the water and ruffle his feathers.

As we approach the end of another millennium of gardening, take time to remember the great gardening years in your past (and the less-than-great ones, too!). Flip back through your old calendars and records and see how far you've come.

As we look toward the new millennium, with all its challenges and discoveries, think about how you can become the inspiration for a whole new crop of gardeners—by sharing your knowledge, experiences, and enthusiasm with your family, friends, neighbors, and community.

Happy gardening!

Heidi Stonehill

Heidi Stonehill
Editor

P.S. If you have a tip you'd like me to consider for possible publication in a future edition of the calendar, or if you have comments or suggestions, drop me a note by writing to:

Heidi Stonehill, Calendar Editor
Rodale Garden Books
Rodale Press, Inc.
33 East Minor Street
Emmaus, PA 18098-0099
or e-mail hstoneh1@rodalepress.com

If you want to order additional copies of this calendar for friends or family or are interested in any of our Rodale Garden Books, call 1-800-848-4735.

🐦 **15** Friday

☐ ☐
HIGH LOW

🐦 **16** Saturday

☐ ☐
HIGH LOW

🐦 **17** Sunday ●

☐ ☐
HIGH LOW

🐦 **NOTES**

December	January	February
S M T W T F S	S M T W T F S	S M T W T F S
1 2 3 4 5	1 2	1 2 3 4 5 6
6 7 8 9 10 11 12	3 4 5 6 7 8 9	7 8 9 10 11 12 13
13 14 15 16 17 18 19	10 11 12 13 14 15 16	14 15 16 17 18 19 20
20 21 22 23 24 25 26	17 18 19 20 21 22 23	21 22 23 24 25 26 27
27 28 29 30 31	24 25 26 27 28 29 30	28
	31	

JANUARY

Keep rambunctious bamboo from running rampant by trenching them at planting time. Dig a 30-inch-deep trench that's wide enough to hold your plants. Angle the sides of the trench outward at a 45 degree angle. Use tough, synthetic landscape fabric or a heavy-duty commercial edging to line the sides of the trench, extending the material 5 inches above the trench rim. When the bamboo runners hit the sides of the trench, they'll bend upward and emerge within the original clump.

 18 Monday

☐ ☐
HIGH LOW

• *Martin Luther King Jr. Day*

 19 Tuesday

☐ ☐
HIGH LOW

 20 Wednesday

☐ ☐
HIGH LOW

21 Thursday

☐ ☐
HIGH LOW

 **22** Friday

 23 Saturday

 24 Sunday

 NOTES

December	January	February
S M T W T F S	S M T W T F S	S M T W T F S
1 2 3 4 5	1 2	1 2 3 4 5 6
6 7 8 9 10 11 12	3 4 5 6 7 8 9	7 8 9 10 11 12 13
13 14 15 16 17 18 19	10 11 12 13 14 15 16	14 15 16 17 18 19 20
20 21 22 23 24 25 26	17 18 19 20 21 22 23	21 22 23 24 25 26 27
27 28 29 30 31	24 25 26 27 28 29 30	28
	31	

JANUARY

Just what is El Niño? About every 3 to 5 years, the trade winds diminish, and warm water in the western Pacific Ocean is then able to travel along the equator toward the East. This causes changes in weather patterns and other effects across the world. In North America, we may see higher than normal temperatures in western Canada and the north central United States and cooler temperatures in the southern United States. Heavier precipitation often falls in California and the southern United States.

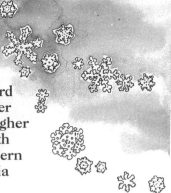

 25 Monday

HIGH   LOW

 26 Tuesday

HIGH   LOW

27 Wednesday

HIGH   LOW

28 Thursday

HIGH   LOW

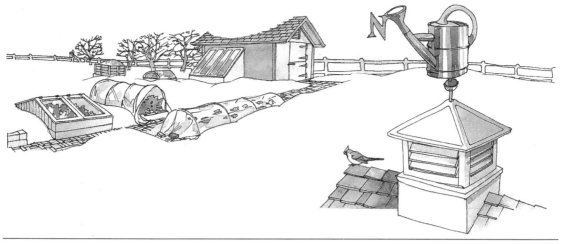

 **29** Friday

HIGH LOW

 **30** Saturday

HIGH LOW

 31 Sunday   *Blue Moon*

HIGH LOW

 NOTES

December	January	February
S M T W T F S	S M T W T F S	S M T W T F S
1 2 3 4 5	1 2	1 2 3 4 5 6
6 7 8 9 10 11 12	3 4 5 6 7 8 9	7 8 9 10 11 12 13
13 14 15 16 17 18 19	10 11 12 13 14 15 16	14 15 16 17 18 19 20
20 21 22 23 24 25 26	17 18 19 20 21 22 23	21 22 23 24 25 26 27
27 28 29 30 31	24 25 26 27 28 29 30	28
	31	

FEBRUARY

Keep an eye out for groundhogs emerging from hibernation in late winter and early spring. Their winter burrows include a small hibernation chamber with a grassy, leafy nest. The main entrance is surrounded by mounds of earth; other exits may exist as well. Winter burrows are often located in protected places, such as on slopes in brushy or wooded areas. Groundhogs rarely use these burrows other than in the winter, preferring other, often more expansive, burrows for the warmer seasons.

---

1 Monday
25°

HIGH LOW

---

2 Tuesday

I missed quit a few days - we've been so busy between wood & Tyler!! I just haven't taken the time to write. Yesterday I worked out my plans for the vegetable garden + the field. I think I have all the seed I need - except field corn.

• Groundhog Day • Candlemas Day about 5°

HIGH LOW

---

3 Wednesday

HIGH LOW

---

4 Thursday ~10°

did wood this morning - very cold out - went to M+D to clean - saw baby SADie - need to clean + organize tomorrow.

HIGH LOW

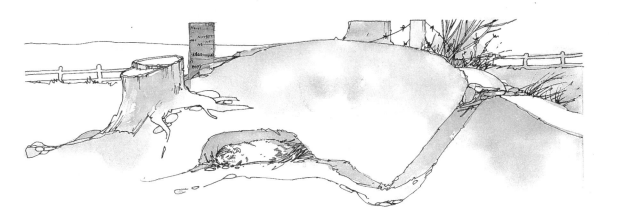

 5 Friday

HIGH LOW

 6 Saturday

HIGH LOW

 7 Sunday

HIGH LOW

 NOTES

January						
S	M	T	W	T	F	S
					1	2
3	4	5	6	7	8	9
10	11	12	13	14	15	16
17	18	19	20	21	22	23
24	25	26	27	28	29	30
31						

February						
S	M	T	W	T	F	S
	1	2	3	4	5	6
7	8	9	10	11	12	13
14	15	16	17	18	19	20
21	22	23	24	25	26	27
28						

March						
S	M	T	W	T	F	S
	1	2	3	4	5	6
7	8	9	10	11	12	13
14	15	16	17	18	19	20
21	22	23	24	25	26	27
28	29	30	31			

FEBRUARY

Through the ages, plants have taken on many meanings.
Use the language of flowers to compose your own valentine message:
crocuses—mirth or cheerfulness; ferns—sincerity or fascination;
forget-me-nots—true love or don't forget me; pansies—you occupy
my thoughts; marjoram—blushes; periwinkle—friendship; red
roses—love; stock—lasting beauty; sweet William—gallantry; tulips—
declaration of love; and violets—faithfulness and modesty.

---

 8   Monday

HIGH   LOW

---

 9   Tuesday

HIGH   LOW

---

10   Wednesday

HIGH   LOW

---

11   Thursday

HIGH   LOW

 12 Friday

HIGH LOW

• *Lincoln's Birthday*

 13 Saturday

HIGH LOW

 14 Sunday

HIGH LOW

• *Valentine's Day*

 NOTES

January						
S	M	T	W	T	F	S
					1	2
3	4	5	6	7	8	9
10	11	12	13	14	15	16
17	18	19	20	21	22	23
24	25	26	27	28	29	30
31						

February						
S	M	T	W	T	F	S
	1	2	3	4	5	6
7	8	9	10	11	12	13
14	15	16	17	18	19	20
21	22	23	24	25	26	27
28						

March						
S	M	T	W	T	F	S
	1	2	3	4	5	6
7	8	9	10	11	12	13
14	15	16	17	18	19	20
21	22	23	24	25	26	27
28	29	30	31			

FEBRUARY

Why not celebrate Valentine's Day all year by planting a garden full of plants with heart-shaped leaves? In partial shade, plants like European wild ginger, Serbian bellflower, red epimedium, 'Frances Williams' hosta, and woolly blue violet will put some "heart" in your planting.

 15 Monday

HIGH LOW

• *Presidents' Day*

 16 Tuesday ●

HIGH LOW

---

17 Wednesday

HIGH LOW

• *Ash Wednesday*

 18 Thursday

HIGH LOW

 19 Friday

 20 Saturday

 21 Sunday

 NOTES

January								February								March					
S	M	T	W	T	F	S		S	M	T	W	T	F	S		S	M	T	W	T	F	S
					1	2			1	2	3	4	5	6			1	2	3	4	5	6
3	4	5	6	7	8	9		7	8	9	10	11	12	13		7	8	9	10	11	12	13
10	11	12	13	14	15	16		14	15	16	17	18	19	20		14	15	16	17	18	19	20
17	18	19	20	21	22	23		21	22	23	24	25	26	27		21	22	23	24	25	26	27
24	25	26	27	28	29	30		28								28	29	30	31			
31																						

FEBRUARY

One of the joys of vegetable growing is harvesting lots of ripe, juicy tomatoes. One of the headaches is fighting tomato diseases. If verticillium and fusarium wilts are prevalent in your area, ensure a successful harvest by buying disease-resistant plants. In catalogs, look for a V (for verticillium resistance) and F or FF (for resistance to various fusarium races) next to the name. Plants like 'Super Roma' VF or 'Mountain Delight' VFF should withstand these diseases.

 22 Monday

HIGH   LOW

• *Washington's Birthday*

 23 Tuesday

HIGH   LOW

24 Wednesday

HIGH   LOW

25 Thursday

HIGH   LOW

 26 Friday

HIGH LOW

 27 Saturday

HIGH LOW

 28 Sunday

HIGH LOW

 NOTES

January						
S	M	T	W	T	F	S
					1	2
3	4	5	6	7	8	9
10	11	12	13	14	15	16
17	18	19	20	21	22	23
24	25	26	27	28	29	30
31						

February						
S	M	T	W	T	F	S
	1	2	3	4	5	6
7	8	9	10	11	12	13
14	15	16	17	18	19	20
21	22	23	24	25	26	27
28						

March						
S	M	T	W	T	F	S
	1	2	3	4	5	6
7	8	9	10	11	12	13
14	15	16	17	18	19	20
21	22	23	24	25	26	27
28	29	30	31			

MARCH

Think twice before adding diseased plants and leaves to
the compost pile. Although hot composting temperatures
can kill plant diseases like botrytis, others survive.
If you don't want to take a chance on spreading a
disease throughout your garden, you might try burning
the plant material and then adding the ashes to your
compost instead. Otherwise, throw diseased plants
out with the garbage.

---

1 Monday
HIGH LOW

Oh-oh - March came in like a lamb!

---

2 Tuesday ☺ *Sap Moon*
HIGH LOW

---

3 Wednesday
HIGH LOW

---

4 Thursday
HIGH LOW

Got our Nanny goats today!
(2) Thelma & Louise - both are supposed
to be bred - but don't know when!
(they were given to us!)

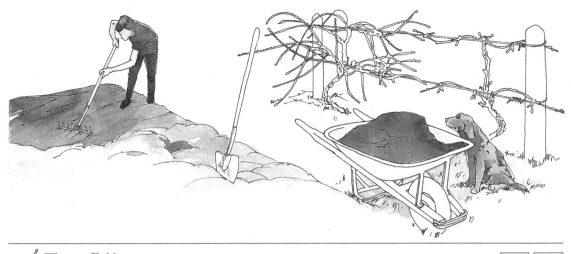

5 Friday

HIGH LOW

6 Saturday

HIGH LOW

Think we found some pigs today —
will know for sure tonite.
Baked bread this morning

(supposed to get to −5° tonite !!)

7 Sunday

HIGH LOW

PICKED UP PIGS 1 BOAR, 2 GILTS, 2 BARROWS

NOTES

MARCH

Heirloom today, gone tomorrow? Not if we keep growing plants from the past. Whether our goal is to enjoy old-time flavor, protect genetic diversity, try unusual varieties, preserve history, continue family traditions, or relive special memories, growing heirloom plants adds value and enjoyment to our gardens. Look for heirloom plants in specialty seed catalogs, contact seed-saving organizations, and ask your family and friends!

---

8   Monday

HIGH   LOW

• *Commonwealth Day (Canada)*

9   Tuesday

HIGH   LOW

---

10   Wednesday ☽

HIGH   LOW

---

11   Thursday

HIGH   LOW

 12 Friday

HIGH LOW

 13 Saturday

HIGH LOW

 14 Sunday

HIGH LOW

 NOTES

February						
S	M	T	W	T	F	S
	1	2	3	4	5	6
7	8	9	10	11	12	13
14	15	16	17	18	19	20
21	22	23	24	25	26	27
28						

March						
S	M	T	W	T	F	S
	1	2	3	4	5	6
7	8	9	10	11	12	13
14	15	16	17	18	19	20
21	22	23	24	25	26	27
28	29	30	31			

April						
S	M	T	W	T	F	S
					1	2	3
4	5	6	7	8	9	10
11	12	13	14	15	16	17
18	19	20	21	22	23	24
25	26	27	28	29	30	

MARCH

"I hardly ever use a shovel for planting anymore," says Deb Martin, of Allentown, Pennsylvania. "My mattock makes it so quick and easy to dig a nice-sized hole for anything I want to plant." The mattock's hoe end breaks through shale and sod, while the ax end cuts through thick roots. "Using a mattock is a great stress buster, too—you can really release some tension as you swing it over your head and thunk! into the soil." Afterward, use a digging fork to loosen the soil in and around the planting hole.

15   Monday

HIGH   LOW

---

16   Tuesday

HIGH   LOW

---

17   Wednesday ●

HIGH   LOW

• *St. Patrick's Day*

---

18   Thursday

HIGH   LOW

 19 Friday

HIGH   LOW

• *Swallows Day, when the birds return to San Juan Capistrano Mission in California*

 20 Saturday

HIGH   LOW

• *Spring begins at 8:46 P.M.*

21 Sunday

HIGH   LOW

 NOTES

February						
S	M	T	W	T	F	S
	1	2	3	4	5	6
7	8	9	10	11	12	13
14	15	16	17	18	19	20
21	22	23	24	25	26	27
28						

March						
S	M	T	W	T	F	S
	1	2	3	4	5	6
7	8	9	10	11	12	13
14	15	16	17	18	19	20
21	22	23	24	25	26	27
28	29	30	31			

April						
S	M	T	W	T	F	S
					1	2	3
4	5	6	7	8	9	10
11	12	13	14	15	16	17
18	19	20	21	22	23	24
25	26	27	28	29	30	

MARCH

To make an arbor that's cheaper than a store-bought metal one, Nancy Ondra, owner of Pendragon Perennials, finds her supplies in the plumbing section of the hardware store. Using a tubing cutter, she cuts ½-inch copper water piping to the desired length for her design, attaches appropriate fittings, and secures the joints with plumber's adhesive like Plumber's Goop. The result is a sturdy arbor for her flowering vines.

---

22 Monday

HIGH   LOW

---

23 Tuesday

HIGH   LOW

---

24 Wednesday 🌙

HIGH   LOW

---

25 Thursday

HIGH   LOW

 26 Friday

 27 Saturday

HIGH LOW

• *Robert D. Rodale (1930–1990) born; author, editor, company chairman, and international promoter of organic gardening and regenerative agriculture*

 28 Sunday

HIGH LOW

• *Palm Sunday*

 NOTES

February	March	April
S M T W T F S	S M T W T F S	S M T W T F S
1 2 3 4 5 6	1 2 3 4 5 6	1 2 3
7 8 9 10 11 12 13	7 8 9 10 11 12 13	4 5 6 7 8 9 10
14 15 16 17 18 19 20	14 15 16 17 18 19 20	11 12 13 14 15 16 17
21 22 23 24 25 26 27	21 22 23 24 25 26 27	18 19 20 21 22 23 24
28	28 29 30 31	25 26 27 28 29 30

MARCH · APRIL

There is a blessing in the air,
Which seems a sense of joy to yield
To the bare trees, and mountains bare,
And grass in the green field.
                    —William Wordsworth

---

 29   Monday

HIGH   LOW

---

 30   Tuesday

HIGH   LOW

---

 31   Wednesday   *Blue Moon*

HIGH   LOW

• *Passover begins at sundown*

---

1   Thursday

HIGH   LOW

• *April Fools' Day*

 2   Friday   .

                                            HIGH   LOW

• *Good Friday*

 3   Saturday   HIGH   LOW

 4   Sunday   HIGH   LOW

• *Easter* • *Daylight Savings Time begins at 2:00* A.M.

 NOTES

February							March							April						
S	M	T	W	T	F	S	S	M	T	W	T	F	S	S	M	T	W	T	F	S
	1	2	3	4	5	6		1	2	3	4	5	6						1	2	3
7	8	9	10	11	12	13	7	8	9	10	11	12	13	4	5	6	7	8	9	10
14	15	16	17	18	19	20	14	15	16	17	18	19	20	11	12	13	14	15	16	17
21	22	23	24	25	26	27	21	22	23	24	25	26	27	18	19	20	21	22	23	24
28							28	29	30	31				25	26	27	28	29	30

APRIL

For a striking plant combination, grow a few clumps of little quaking grass (*Briza minor*) in front of a plant or two of tall flame grass (*Miscanthus sinensis* 'Purpurascens'). Choose goldmoss stonecrop and Kamschatka sedum as groundcovers. In summer, you'll have a sea of different greens, with the groundcovers in bloom. In fall, the graceful flame grass seedheads top reddish leaves that echo the red tint of the groundcovers.

 5   Monday

HIGH   LOW

 6   Tuesday

HIGH   LOW

7   Wednesday

HIGH   LOW

 8   Thursday

HIGH   LOW

9 Friday

☐ ☐
HIGH LOW

10 Saturday

☐ ☐
HIGH LOW

11 Sunday

☐ ☐
HIGH LOW

NOTES

March						
S	M	T	W	T	F	S
		1	2	3	4	5	6
7	8	9	10	11	12	13
14	15	16	17	18	19	20
21	22	23	24	25	26	27
28	29	30	31			

April						
S	M	T	W	T	F	S
				1	2	3
4	5	6	7	8	9	10
11	12	13	14	15	16	17
18	19	20	21	22	23	24
25	26	27	28	29	30	

May						
S	M	T	W	T	F	S
						1
2	3	4	5	6	7	8
9	10	11	12	13	14	15
16	17	18	19	20	21	22
23	24	25	26	27	28	29
30	31					

APRIL

Scented geraniums come in a wide range of leaf shapes and textures, with plenty of scents to choose from—including rose, lemon, mint, orange, strawberry, apple, coconut, and spicy nutmeg. Just brush or gently crush the leaves and revel in the aroma. The leaves will keep their fragrance when dried, so they're great for potpourri and other crafts!

---

 12 Monday

HIGH LOW

---

 13 Tuesday

HIGH LOW

• *Thomas Jefferson (1743–1826) born*

14 Wednesday

HIGH LOW

---

15 Thursday

HIGH LOW

🍃 **16** Friday ⬤

🍃 **17** Saturday

HIGH LOW

🍃 **18** Sunday

HIGH LOW

🍃 NOTES

March						
S	M	T	W	T	F	S
		1	2	3	4	5	6
7	8	9	10	11	12	13
14	15	16	17	18	19	20
21	22	23	24	25	26	27
28	29	30	31			

April						
S	M	T	W	T	F	S
					1	2	3
4	5	6	7	8	9	10
11	12	13	14	15	16	17
18	19	20	21	22	23	24
25	26	27	28	29	30	

May						
S	M	T	W	T	F	S
						1
2	3	4	5	6	7	8
9	10	11	12	13	14	15
16	17	18	19	20	21	22
23	24	25	26	27	28	29
30	31					

APRIL

Outmaneuver northern root-knot nematodes by rotating susceptible plants with resistant perennials. The perennials keep the nematode populations down so your vulnerable crops can thrive. First, grow perennials like asters, butterfly weed, sweet William, purple coneflowers, or lilyturf for one year in your garden plot. Then transplant them to another site, and plant your susceptible plants, like tomatoes, in the old spot.

19 Monday

HIGH LOW

• *Lyrids meteor shower visible, peaking around the 21st or 22nd, with an average of 16 meteors per hour*

20 Tuesday

HIGH LOW

---

21 Wednesday

HIGH LOW

---

22 Thursday

HIGH LOW

 **23** Friday

HIGH   LOW

 **24** Saturday

HIGH   LOW

25 Sunday

HIGH   LOW

NOTES

March						
S	M	T	W	T	F	S
	1	2	3	4	5	6
7	8	9	10	11	12	13
14	15	16	17	18	19	20
21	22	23	24	25	26	27
28	29	30	31			

April						
S	M	T	W	T	F	S
				1	2	3
4	5	6	7	8	9	10
11	12	13	14	15	16	17
18	19	20	21	22	23	24
25	26	27	28	29	30	

May						
S	M	T	W	T	F	S
						1
2	3	4	5	6	7	8
9	10	11	12	13	14	15
16	17	18	19	20	21	22
23	24	25	26	27	28	29
30	31					

APRIL · MAY

The refreshing lemon scent of lemon verbena makes it a must for any fragrance or craft garden. It's only hardy to Zone 9, so you'll need to grow this shrub in cooler climates as a container plant and then bring it indoors for the winter. Use the dried, crushed leaves to flavor marinades, salad dressings, and beverages. You can also use fresh leaves in recipes, but remove them before serving since they can be tough. The leaves also work well in potpourris and sachets.

 26 Monday

HIGH LOW

• *John James Audubon (1785–1851) born*

 27 Tuesday

HIGH LOW

28 Wednesday

HIGH LOW

29 Thursday

HIGH LOW

30 Friday ☽ *Seed Moon*

HIGH LOW

1 Saturday

HIGH LOW

2 Sunday

HIGH LOW

NOTES

March						
S	M	T	W	T	F	S
		1	2	3	4	5	6
7	8	9	10	11	12	13
14	15	16	17	18	19	20
21	22	23	24	25	26	27
28	29	30	31			

April						
S	M	T	W	T	F	S
				1	2	3
4	5	6	7	8	9	10
11	12	13	14	15	16	17
18	19	20	21	22	23	24
25	26	27	28	29	30	

May						
S	M	T	W	T	F	S
						1
2	3	4	5	6	7	8
9	10	11	12	13	14	15
16	17	18	19	20	21	22
23	24	25	26	27	28	29
30	31					

MAY

May, with alle thy floures and thy grene,
Welcome be thou, faire, fresshe May.
                                    —Chaucer

 3   Monday   HIGH   LOW

4   Tuesday   HIGH   LOW

5   Wednesday   HIGH   LOW

6   Thursday   HIGH   LOW

7 Friday

8 Saturday

HIGH LOW

9 Sunday

HIGH LOW

• *Mother's Day*

NOTES

April	May	June
S M T W T F S	S M T W T F S	S M T W T F S
1 2 3	1	1 2 3 4 5
4 5 6 7 8 9 10	2 3 4 5 6 7 8	6 7 8 9 10 11 12
11 12 13 14 15 16 17	9 10 11 12 13 14 15	13 14 15 16 17 18 19
18 19 20 21 22 23 24	16 17 18 19 20 21 22	20 21 22 23 24 25 26
25 26 27 28 29 30	23 24 25 26 27 28 29	27 28 29 30
	30 31	

MAY

If you see a large woodpecker feeding on the ground in spring, chances are it's a common flicker. This white-rumped bird inhabits most of North America. It has three major color variations, depending on what part of the country it lives in. It eats more ants than any other North American bird, but it will also gulp down other insects, as well as fruits, seeds, and nuts, especially in fall and winter. You can hear the wick, wick, wick, wick or flick-a, flick-a, flick-a calls of the males in spring.

 10 Monday

☐ HIGH ☐ LOW

11 Tuesday

☐ HIGH ☐ LOW

12 Wednesday

☐ HIGH ☐ LOW

13 Thursday

☐ HIGH ☐ LOW

14 Friday

HIGH	LOW

15 Saturday ●

HIGH	LOW

• *Armed Forces Day*

16 Sunday

HIGH	LOW

NOTES

April	May	June
S M T W T F S	S M T W T F S	S M T W T F S
1 2 3	1	1 2 3 4 5
4 5 6 7 8 9 10	2 3 4 5 6 7 8	6 7 8 9 10 11 12
11 12 13 14 15 16 17	9 10 11 12 13 14 15	13 14 15 16 17 18 19
18 19 20 21 22 23 24	16 17 18 19 20 21 22	20 21 22 23 24 25 26
25 26 27 28 29 30	23 24 25 26 27 28 29	27 28 29 30
	30 31	

MAY

Butterfly boxes offer shelter for hibernating butterflies, although you may find that they prefer more natural sites. To encourage butterflies to use your butterfly box, Delilah Smittle of Allentown, Pennsylvania, suggests lining the inside of your butterfly boxes with tree bark from fallen logs. "The butterflies will have the same kind of material to cling to as they do when they find places to hibernate in knotholes and along the sides of tree trunks."

---

17   Monday

HIGH   LOW

---

18   Tuesday

HIGH   LOW

---

19   Wednesday

HIGH   LOW

---

20   Thursday

HIGH   LOW

 21 Friday

HIGH　LOW

 22 Saturday

HIGH　LOW

 23 Sunday

HIGH　LOW

 NOTES

	April					
S	M	T	W	T	F	S
					1	2	3
4	5	6	7	8	9	10
11	12	13	14	15	16	17
18	19	20	21	22	23	24
25	26	27	28	29	30	

	May					
S	M	T	W	T	F	S
						1
2	3	4	5	6	7	8
9	10	11	12	13	14	15
16	17	18	19	20	21	22
23	24	25	26	27	28	29
30	31					

	June					
S	M	T	W	T	F	S
		1	2	3	4	5
6	7	8	9	10	11	12
13	14	15	16	17	18	19
20	21	22	23	24	25	26
27	28	29	30			

MAY

Add interest to your lawn with herbs. If you have cold winters and your summers don't get broiling hot, you can interplant tough herbs like Roman chamomile, pennyroyal, creeping thyme, and common yarrow in your lawn. These plants tolerate weekly mowing, can take the competition from lawn grass, and form fragrant, attractive mats of foliage.

 24 Monday

HIGH LOW

• *Victoria Day (Canada)*

25 Tuesday

HIGH LOW

 26 Wednesday

HIGH LOW

27 Thursday

HIGH LOW

Rachel Carson (1907–1964) born; author of Silent Spring

28 Friday

HIGH LOW

29 Saturday

HIGH LOW

30 Sunday 🌙 *Planting Moon*

HIGH LOW

NOTES

April						
S	M	T	W	T	F	S
					1	2	3
4	5	6	7	8	9	10
11	12	13	14	15	16	17
18	19	20	21	22	23	24
25	26	27	28	29	30	

May						
S	M	T	W	T	F	S
						1
2	3	4	5	6	7	8
9	10	11	12	13	14	15
16	17	18	19	20	21	22
23	24	25	26	27	28	29
30	31					

June						
S	M	T	W	T	F	S
		1	2	3	4	5
6	7	8	9	10	11	12
13	14	15	16	17	18	19
20	21	22	23	24	25	26
27	28	29	30			

MAY · JUNE

Are June beetles and Japanese beetles the same? June beetles include about 200 species of ½- to 1-inch-long brown or black beetles. The ¼- to ½-inch-long Japanese beetle is only one species and is a metallic blue-green with copper wing covers. Adult June beetles emerge around April or May, while Japanese beetles appear in May or June. Most adult June beetles feed at night on tree foliage. Japanese beetles feed in the day on a wide range of ornamentals and edibles.

---

 31 Monday

HIGH   LOW

• *Memorial Day (observed)*

 1 Tuesday

HIGH   LOW

---

 2 Wednesday

HIGH   LOW

---

3 Thursday

HIGH   LOW

June Beetles

Japanese Beetles

---

4 Friday

HIGH ☐ LOW ☐

---

5 Saturday

HIGH ☐ LOW ☐

---

6 Sunday

HIGH ☐ LOW ☐

NOTES

April						
S	M	T	W	T	F	S
				1	2	3
4	5	6	7	8	9	10
11	12	13	14	15	16	17
18	19	20	21	22	23	24
25	26	27	28	29	30	

May						
S	M	T	W	T	F	S
						1
2	3	4	5	6	7	8
9	10	11	12	13	14	15
16	17	18	19	20	21	22
23	24	25	26	27	28	29
30	31					

June						
S	M	T	W	T	F	S
		1	2	3	4	5
6	7	8	9	10	11	12
13	14	15	16	17	18	19
20	21	22	23	24	25	26
27	28	29	30			

JUNE

Make your evening in the garden magical by setting the mood with well-placed lighting. Shine low lights down onto pathways, spotlight a favorite tree, or direct lights up through delicate shrub foliage. Aim lights along the side of a fence to emphasize its texture. Silhouette an interesting sculpture, make shadows against a wall, or produce other enchanting effects. Be creative and have fun!

 7   Monday   HIGH   LOW

 8   Tuesday   HIGH   LOW

9   Wednesday   HIGH   LOW

 10   Thursday   HIGH   LOW

 11 Friday

HIGH   LOW

 12 Saturday

HIGH   LOW

 13 Sunday ●

HIGH   LOW

 NOTES

	May					
S	M	T	W	T	F	S
						1
2	3	4	5	6	7	8
9	10	11	12	13	14	15
16	17	18	19	20	21	22
23	24	25	26	27	28	29
30	31					

	June					
S	M	T	W	T	F	S
		1	2	3	4	5
6	7	8	9	10	11	12
13	14	15	16	17	18	19
20	21	22	23	24	25	26
27	28	29	30			

	July					
S	M	T	W	T	F	S
				1	2	3
4	5	6	7	8	9	10
11	12	13	14	15	16	17
18	19	20	21	22	23	24
25	26	27	28	29	30	31

JUNE

Capsaicinoids—even the name sounds painful. These are a group of compounds (capsaicin being the most common) in chili peppers that give them their popular blistering-hot taste. Remember, if you bite into a pepper that's too hot to handle, don't reach for the water jug—that will just spread the fire around. Try milk, yogurt, or a teaspoon of sugar instead.

14 Monday

HIGH   LOW

• Flag Day • Ruth Stout (1884–1980) born; originated permanent mulch method of gardening

15 Tuesday

HIGH   LOW

16 Wednesday

HIGH   LOW

17 Thursday

HIGH   LOW

18 Friday

HIGH   LOW

19 Saturday

HIGH   LOW

20 Sunday

HIGH   LOW

• *Father's Day*

NOTES

	May							June							July					
S	M	T	W	T	F	S	S	M	T	W	T	F	S	S	M	T	W	T	F	S
						1			1	2	3	4	5					1	2	3
2	3	4	5	6	7	8	6	7	8	9	10	11	12	4	5	6	7	8	9	10
9	10	11	12	13	14	15	13	14	15	16	17	18	19	11	12	13	14	15	16	17
16	17	18	19	20	21	22	20	21	22	23	24	25	26	18	19	20	21	22	23	24
23	24	25	26	27	28	29	27	28	29	30				25	26	27	28	29	30	31
30	31																			

JUNE

Warm summer weather often means parched plants. Tend to your plants' needs while saving water by installing drip irrigation or soaker hoses for efficient watering and using a moisture sensor to determine when more water is needed. Collect rainwater for your garden by placing a barrel under a downspout. Apply mulch to keep the soil moist, and routinely get rid of water-slurping weeds. And make sure you choose drought-tolerant plants if summers are usually dry.

 **21** Monday

HIGH LOW

• *Summer begins at 3:49 P.M.*

 **22** Tuesday

HIGH LOW

23 Wednesday

HIGH LOW

24 Thursday

HIGH LOW

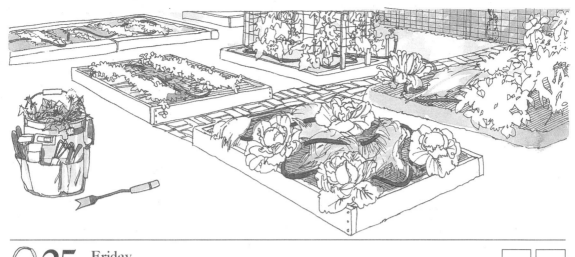

 25 Friday

HIGH LOW

 26 Saturday

HIGH LOW

 27 Sunday

HIGH LOW

 NOTES

	May							June							July					
S	M	T	W	T	F	S	S	M	T	W	T	F	S	S	M	T	W	T	F	S
						1			1	2	3	4	5						1	2	3
2	3	4	5	6	7	8	6	7	8	9	10	11	12	4	5	6	7	8	9	10
9	10	11	12	13	14	15	13	14	15	16	17	18	19	11	12	13	14	15	16	17
16	17	18	19	20	21	22	20	21	22	23	24	25	26	18	19	20	21	22	23	24
23	24	25	26	27	28	29	27	28	29	30				25	26	27	28	29	30	31
30	31																			

JUNE · JULY

In the 1760s, before the American Revolution, the Sons of Liberty met in Boston near an elm known as the "Liberty Tree." Because the tree was an emblem of freedom for the rebelling colonists, British soldiers cut the tree down in 1775. Today you can plant an 'American Liberty' elm, named in honor of that famous Boston tree and resistant to the devastating Dutch elm disease. For more information about these beautiful trees, write to: Elm Research Institute, Elm Street, Westmoreland, NH 03467.

 28 Monday   ☺ *Rose Moon*

HIGH   LOW

29 Tuesday

HIGH   LOW

30 Wednesday

HIGH   LOW

1 Thursday

HIGH   LOW

• *Canada Day*

 2   Friday

HIGH   LOW

 3   Saturday

HIGH   LOW

 4   Sunday

HIGH   LOW

• *Independence Day*

 NOTES

May								June								July						
S	M	T	W	T	F	S		S	M	T	W	T	F	S		S	M	T	W	T	F	S
						1				1	2	3	4	5						1	2	3
2	3	4	5	6	7	8		6	7	8	9	10	11	12		4	5	6	7	8	9	10
9	10	11	12	13	14	15		13	14	15	16	17	18	19		11	12	13	14	15	16	17
16	17	18	19	20	21	22		20	21	22	23	24	25	26		18	19	20	21	22	23	24
23	24	25	26	27	28	29		27	28	29	30					25	26	27	28	29	30	31
30	31																					

JULY

A nighttime garden makes summer evenings even more enjoyable. As dusk approaches, you can watch your flowers open, relish the intensifying fragrance, and admire the pale petals that glow in the fading light. Plants like showy moonflower vine, fragrant evening stock, colorful four-o'clocks, and night-blooming evening primroses are sure to delight you and your guests. You can also try nocturnal varieties of daylilies, such as 'Moon Frolic' or 'Puddin.'

---

 5   Monday

HIGH   LOW

---

 6   Tuesday

HIGH   LOW

---

7   Wednesday

HIGH   LOW

---

 8   Thursday

HIGH   LOW

 9 Friday

HIGH   LOW

 10 Saturday

HIGH   LOW

 11 Sunday

HIGH   LOW

 NOTES

June						
S	M	T	W	T	F	S
		1	2	3	4	5
6	7	8	9	10	11	12
13	14	15	16	17	18	19
20	21	22	23	24	25	26
27	28	29	30			

July						
S	M	T	W	T	F	S
				1	2	3
4	5	6	7	8	9	10
11	12	13	14	15	16	17
18	19	20	21	22	23	24
25	26	27	28	29	30	31

August						
S	M	T	W	T	F	S
1	2	3	4	5	6	7
8	9	10	11	12	13	14
15	16	17	18	19	20	21
22	23	24	25	26	27	28
29	30	31				

JULY

When do you plant fall vegetables? For each crop, add up the days to maturity plus the days to germination and days to transplanting (if any). Then tack on a short-day factor of 14 to compensate for the cooler, shorter days. For frost-tender crops like cucumbers, add another 14 days. Take the total and count back from your average first fall frost date to find out when to plant your seeds. See "How to Figure the Last Planting Date" in the back of this calendar for more tips.

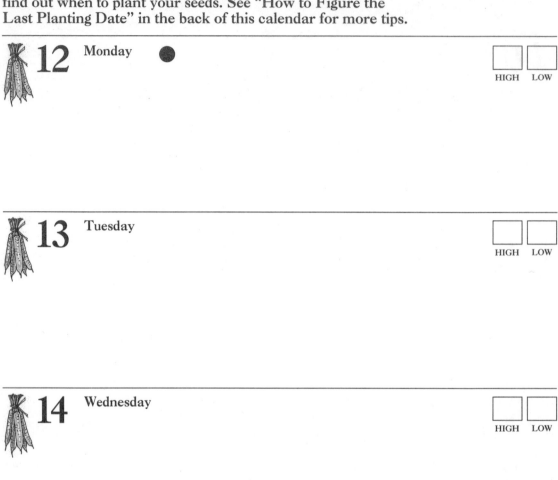

---

12 Monday ●

HIGH   LOW

---

13 Tuesday

HIGH   LOW

---

14 Wednesday

HIGH   LOW

---

15 Thursday

HIGH   LOW

 16 Friday

HIGH   LOW

 17 Saturday

HIGH   LOW

 18 Sunday

HIGH   LOW

 NOTES

June						
S	M	T	W	T	F	S
		1	2	3	4	5
6	7	8	9	10	11	12
13	14	15	16	17	18	19
20	21	22	23	24	25	26
27	28	29	30			

July						
S	M	T	W	T	F	S
				1	2	3
4	5	6	7	8	9	10
11	12	13	14	15	16	17
18	19	20	21	22	23	24
25	26	27	28	29	30	31

August						
S	M	T	W	T	F	S
1	2	3	4	5	6	7
8	9	10	11	12	13	14
15	16	17	18	19	20	21
22	23	24	25	26	27	28
29	30	31				

JULY

For a hard-to-pull, deep-rooted perennial weed, soak the ground around it, and then heave-ho! If that doesn't work, dig carefully around the roots, then lift the plant out. Try not to leave any roots behind, or you may get many weeds where you once had one. If the weed seems to be winning the battle, all is not lost. Clip the weed close to the ground every time green shoots appear. The plant will use up the food stored in its roots and will eventually waste away.

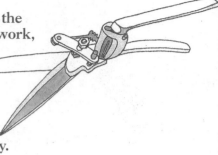

19 Monday

HIGH   LOW

20 Tuesday

HIGH   LOW

21 Wednesday

HIGH   LOW

22 Thursday

HIGH   LOW

 **23** Friday

HIGH   LOW

24 Saturday

HIGH   LOW

25 Sunday

HIGH   LOW

NOTES

June						
S	M	T	W	T	F	S
		1	2	3	4	5
6	7	8	9	10	11	12
13	14	15	16	17	18	19
20	21	22	23	24	25	26
27	28	29	30			

July						
S	M	T	W	T	F	S
				1	2	3
4	5	6	7	8	9	10
11	12	13	14	15	16	17
18	19	20	21	22	23	24
25	26	27	28	29	30	31

August						
S	M	T	W	T	F	S
1	2	3	4	5	6	7
8	9	10	11	12	13	14
15	16	17	18	19	20	21
22	23	24	25	26	27	28
29	30	31				

July · August

Corn smut—those whitish gray blobs that sometimes appear on your corn ears, stems, or tassels—may look unappealing, but it's considered a delicacy in some regions, like Mexico. This unattractive fungus is called *cuitlacoche* or *huitlacoche* in the cooking trade and is grown purposely for gourmet markets. Use cuitlacoche in soups, casseroles, and other dishes calling for cooked mushrooms (which are also fungi, if you recall). Its smoky-sweet flavor tastes like a blend of corn and mushrooms.

 26 Monday

HIGH LOW

 27 Tuesday

HIGH LOW

 28 Wednesday ☺ *Summer Moon*

HIGH LOW

• *Partial lunar eclipse (40%) begins at 6:22 A.M. EDT and ends at 8:46 A.M. EDT. Visible in middle to western North America*

 29 Thursday

HIGH LOW

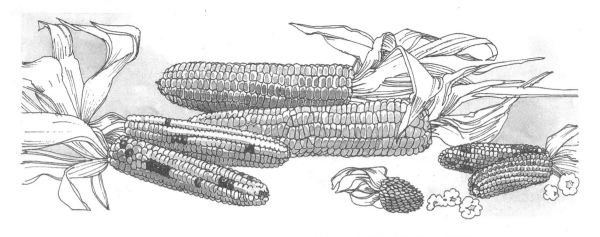

30 Friday

HIGH LOW

31 Saturday

HIGH LOW

1 Sunday

HIGH LOW

 NOTES

June	July	August
S M T W T F S	S M T W T F S	S M T W T F S
1 2 3 4 5	1 2 3	1 2 3 4 5 6 7
6 7 8 9 10 11 12	4 5 6 7 8 9 10	8 9 10 11 12 13 14
13 14 15 16 17 18 19	11 12 13 14 15 16 17	15 16 17 18 19 20 21
20 21 22 23 24 25 26	18 19 20 21 22 23 24	22 23 24 25 26 27 28
27 28 29 30	25 26 27 28 29 30 31	29 30 31

AUGUST

Bullfrogs are the largest frogs in North America, averaging 4 to 7 inches in length. Their booming nighttime "jug-o-rum" calls echo from still or slow-moving water. Usually found along the water's edge, bullfrogs capture insects, worms, crayfish, minnows, fellow frogs, or other unfortunate bite-sized moving objects. These big frogs hibernate in the mud during winter months and can live 7 to 9 years.

2 Monday

HIGH □ LOW □

3 Tuesday

HIGH □ LOW □

4 Wednesday ☾

HIGH □ LOW □

5 Thursday

HIGH □ LOW □

6 Friday

HIGH LOW

7 Saturday

HIGH LOW

8 Sunday

HIGH LOW

NOTES

July						
S	M	T	W	T	F	S
					1	2	3
4	5	6	7	8	9	10
11	12	13	14	15	16	17
18	19	20	21	22	23	24
25	26	27	28	29	30	31

August						
S	M	T	W	T	F	S
1	2	3	4	5	6	7
8	9	10	11	12	13	14
15	16	17	18	19	20	21
22	23	24	25	26	27	28
29	30	31				

September						
S	M	T	W	T	F	S
				1	2	3	4
5	6	7	8	9	10	11
12	13	14	15	16	17	18
19	20	21	22	23	24	25
26	27	28	29	30		

AUGUST

Extend your raspberry season by planting both summer-bearing and everbearing varieties. Cut all of the everbearers' canes to the ground in late fall after fruiting, but prune summerbearers normally. This way you'll have a large midsummer crop from your summerbearers and a single, large late summer or early fall harvest from the everbearers. (Otherwise, with normal pruning, everbearers produce a light fall crop, then an early summer crop the following season.)

---

9   Monday

HIGH   LOW

• *Perseids meteor shower visible, peaking around the 11th or 12th, with an average of 50 meteors per hour*

---

10   Tuesday

HIGH   LOW

---

11   Wednesday ●

HIGH   LOW

---

12   Thursday

HIGH   LOW

 13 Friday

HIGH LOW

 14 Saturday

HIGH LOW

 15 Sunday

HIGH LOW

 NOTES

July	August	September
S M T W T F S	S M T W T F S	S M T W T F S
1 2 3	1 2 3 4 5 6 7	1 2 3 4
4 5 6 7 8 9 10	8 9 10 11 12 13 14	5 6 7 8 9 10 11
11 12 13 14 15 16 17	15 16 17 18 19 20 21	12 13 14 15 16 17 18
18 19 20 21 22 23 24	22 23 24 25 26 27 28	19 20 21 22 23 24 25
25 26 27 28 29 30 31	29 30 31	26 27 28 29 30

AUGUST

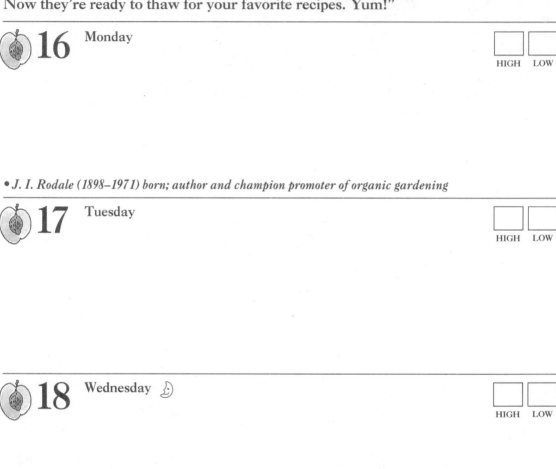

For a fast, easy way to freeze peaches, try this
tip from Fern Bradley of Emmaus, Pennsylvania:
"Arrange ripe (but still firm) whole peaches on a
cookie sheet and put the sheet in the freezer. Wait
several hours or overnight, then remove the tray
from the freezer. Package the frozen peaches in doubled plastic
bags and return them to the deep freeze. To use the peaches,
run warm water over them until the skins slip off in your fingers.
Now they're ready to thaw for your favorite recipes. Yum!"

16 Monday

HIGH LOW

• *J. I. Rodale (1898–1971) born; author and champion promoter of organic gardening*

17 Tuesday

HIGH LOW

18 Wednesday

HIGH LOW

19 Thursday

HIGH LOW

 20 Friday

HIGH LOW

 21 Saturday

HIGH LOW

22 Sunday

HIGH LOW

 NOTES

July	August	September
S M T W T F S	S M T W T F S	S M T W T F S
1 2 3	1 2 3 4 5 6 7	1 2 3 4
4 5 6 7 8 9 10	8 9 10 11 12 13 14	5 6 7 8 9 10 11
11 12 13 14 15 16 17	15 16 17 18 19 20 21	12 13 14 15 16 17 18
18 19 20 21 22 23 24	22 23 24 25 26 27 28	19 20 21 22 23 24 25
25 26 27 28 29 30 31	29 30 31	26 27 28 29 30

AUGUST

Beat the heat with a water garden! Even if you don't have
the time or resources to create a water garden paradise,
you can place a few plants in a plastic tub and enjoy the
soothing effects that a tiny water feature provides.
Submerged plants and plants with leaves that float
on the water's surface will help keep the algae down.
A small waterlily, a few bunches of submerged plants,
two bog plants, and some floating-leaved plants will
thrive in an 18-inch-deep half-barrel container.

 23 Monday

HIGH LOW

 24 Tuesday

HIGH LOW

 25 Wednesday

HIGH LOW

 26 Thursday *Blackberry Patches Moon*

HIGH LOW

 27 Friday

HIGH LOW

 28 Saturday

HIGH LOW

 29 Sunday

HIGH LOW

 NOTES

	July							August							September					
S	M	T	W	T	F	S	S	M	T	W	T	F	S	S	M	T	W	T	F	S
					1	2	3	1	2	3	4	5	6	7					1	2	3	4
4	5	6	7	8	9	10	8	9	10	11	12	13	14	5	6	7	8	9	10	11
11	12	13	14	15	16	17	15	16	17	18	19	20	21	12	13	14	15	16	17	18
18	19	20	21	22	23	24	22	23	24	25	26	27	28	19	20	21	22	23	24	25
25	26	27	28	29	30	31	29	30	31					26	27	28	29	30

AUGUST · SEPTEMBER

Too many tomatoes? Turn them into salsa! Keep a big pitcher of salsa from your favorite recipe in the fridge and pour it into bowls to serve with corn chips when family or guests arrive. For a low-fat snack, cut fresh corn tortillas into wedges with scissors. Lay them out on a cookie sheet sprayed with nonstick vegetable spray and bake them at 350°F until they're crispy. Then dip in!

 30   Monday   HIGH   LOW

 31   Tuesday   HIGH   LOW

 1   Wednesday   HIGH   LOW

 2   Thursday   HIGH   LOW

 3 Friday

HIGH   LOW

4 Saturday

HIGH   LOW

5 Sunday

HIGH   LOW

NOTES

July								August							September						
S	M	T	W	T	F	S		S	M	T	W	T	F	S		S	M	T	W	T	F	S
					1	2	3	1	2	3	4	5	6	7						1	2	3	4
4	5	6	7	8	9	10	8	9	10	11	12	13	14		5	6	7	8	9	10	11
11	12	13	14	15	16	17	15	16	17	18	19	20	21		12	13	14	15	16	17	18
18	19	20	21	22	23	24	22	23	24	25	26	27	28		19	20	21	22	23	24	25
25	26	27	28	29	30	31	29	30	31						26	27	28	29	30

SEPTEMBER

About now, the ruby-throated hummingbird will start its journey from central and eastern North America to southern Mexico and Central America. During the trip, it will normally take a nonstop shortcut across 500 miles of the Gulf of Mexico. To accomplish this astonishing feat, this bundle of energy fattens up on nectar from plants like jewelweed—and from hummingbird feeders— increasing its weight by half. Then it relies on its fat reserves to wing across the ocean.

 6 Monday

HIGH   LOW

• *Labor Day*

 7 Tuesday

HIGH   LOW

 8 Wednesday

HIGH   LOW

 9 Thursday ●

HIGH   LOW

 10 Friday

HIGH LOW

• *Rosh Hashanah begins at sundown*

 11 Saturday

HIGH LOW

 12 Sunday

HIGH LOW

• *Grandparents' Day*

 NOTES

August							September							October						
S	M	T	W	T	F	S	S	M	T	W	T	F	S	S	M	T	W	T	F	S
1	2	3	4	5	6	7				1	2	3	4						1	2
8	9	10	11	12	13	14	5	6	7	8	9	10	11	3	4	5	6	7	8	9
15	16	17	18	19	20	21	12	13	14	15	16	17	18	10	11	12	13	14	15	16
22	23	24	25	26	27	28	19	20	21	22	23	24	25	17	18	19	20	21	22	23
29	30	31					26	27	28	29	30			24	25	26	27	28	29	30
														31						

SEPTEMBER

Avoid fertilizing your perennials once they've stopped actively growing in late summer. The tender leaves and stems produced from fertilizer-induced growth could easily freeze when winter arrives. Instead, let the plants focus their energy on preparing for the colder months ahead.

 13 Monday

HIGH LOW

14 Tuesday

HIGH LOW

15 Wednesday

HIGH LOW

 16 Thursday

 HIGH LOW

 17 Friday

HIGH   LOW

18 Saturday

HIGH   LOW

19 Sunday

HIGH   LOW

• *Yom Kippur begins at sundown*

NOTES

August	September	October
S M T W T F S	S M T W T F S	S M T W T F S
1 2 3 4 5 6 7	1 2 3 4	1 2
8 9 10 11 12 13 14	5 6 7 8 9 10 11	3 4 5 6 7 8 9
15 16 17 18 19 20 21	12 13 14 15 16 17 18	10 11 12 13 14 15 16
22 23 24 25 26 27 28	19 20 21 22 23 24 25	17 18 19 20 21 22 23
29 30 31	26 27 28 29 30	24 25 26 27 28 29 30
		31

SEPTEMBER

If you can't take your clay plant pots inside for the winter, make sure they keep dry. Otherwise, as water absorbed by the pots or the soil inside expands during freezing, your pots will probably crack. Avoid breakage by removing spent plants from each pot and letting the soil dry out thoroughly in fall. Set the pots on top of bricks and wrap the top and sides of each pot with clear plastic, such as a painter's drop cloth. Tie twine around the plastic to hold it in place. Now they're ready for winter's worst!

 20 Monday

HIGH   LOW

 21 Tuesday

HIGH   LOW

 22 Wednesday

HIGH   LOW

 23 Thursday

HIGH   LOW

• *Fall begins at 7:31 P.M.*

24 Friday

HIGH LOW

25 Saturday 🌝 *Harvest Moon*

HIGH LOW

26 Sunday

HIGH LOW

 NOTES

August						
S	M	T	W	T	F	S
1	2	3	4	5	6	7
8	9	10	11	12	13	14
15	16	17	18	19	20	21
22	23	24	25	26	27	28
29	30	31				

September						
S	M	T	W	T	F	S
			1	2	3	4
5	6	7	8	9	10	11
12	13	14	15	16	17	18
19	20	21	22	23	24	25
26	27	28	29	30		

October						
S	M	T	W	T	F	S
					1	2
3	4	5	6	7	8	9
10	11	12	13	14	15	16
17	18	19	20	21	22	23
24	25	26	27	28	29	30
31						

SEPTEMBER • OCTOBER

Now's the time to plant a batch of fall green manure in your garden. Green manures are crops grown for a time and then worked into the soil to increase soil fertility or organic matter content. Good choices for fall include winter rye, Austrian peas, winter wheat, hairy vetch, or barley. Turn them under in early spring before they resume growth.

 27 Monday

HIGH LOW

28 Tuesday

HIGH LOW

29 Wednesday

HIGH LOW

 30 Thursday

HIGH LOW

 1   Friday

HIGH   LOW

 2   Saturday   ☾

HIGH   LOW

 3   Sunday

HIGH   LOW

 NOTES

August	September	October
S M T W T F S	S M T W T F S	S M T W T F S
1 2 3 4 5 6 7	1 2 3 4	1 2
8 9 10 11 12 13 14	5 6 7 8 9 10 11	3 4 5 6 7 8 9
15 16 17 18 19 20 21	12 13 14 15 16 17 18	10 11 12 13 14 15 16
22 23 24 25 26 27 28	19 20 21 22 23 24 25	17 18 19 20 21 22 23
29 30 31	26 27 28 29 30	24 25 26 27 28 29 30
		31

OCTOBER

Fill your fall perennial garden with a riot of color. Pink or white Japanese anemones have single or double flowers that seem to flutter on their slender stems. Boltonias bear many lacy, daisylike pink or white flowers. They look like their relatives, the asters, which bloom in blue, purple, red, pink, or white. Goldenrods give a burst of bright yellow, along with the cheerful yellows of perennial sunflowers and the warm glows of yellow or orange daisylike heleniums.

 4   Monday

HIGH   LOW

 5   Tuesday

HIGH   LOW

6   Wednesday

HIGH   LOW

 7   Thursday

HIGH   LOW

 8 Friday
 HIGH LOW

 9 Saturday
 HIGH LOW

 10 Sunday
 HIGH LOW

 NOTES

September	October	November
S M T W T F S	S M T W T F S	S M T W T F S
1 2 3 4	1 2	1 2 3 4 5 6
5 6 7 8 9 10 11	3 4 5 6 7 8 9	7 8 9 10 11 12 13
12 13 14 15 16 17 18	10 11 12 13 14 15 16	14 15 16 17 18 19 20
19 20 21 22 23 24 25	17 18 19 20 21 22 23	21 22 23 24 25 26 27
26 27 28 29 30	24 25 26 27 28 29 30	28 29 30
	31	

OCTOBER

Protect your bulbs from hungry mice and voles by
surrounding the bulbs with a handful of sharp crushed
gravel at planting time. The creatures will avoid digging
past the sharp objects to reach the bulbs. You don't
have to worry about your daffodils, however. They're
poisonous, and the rodents will wisely keep away.

11 Monday

HIGH   LOW

• Columbus Day (observed) • Thanksgiving (Canada)

12 Tuesday

HIGH   LOW

13 Wednesday

HIGH   LOW

14 Thursday

HIGH   LOW

 15 Friday

HIGH   LOW

 16 Saturday

HIGH   LOW

 17 Sunday

HIGH   LOW

NOTES

September	October	November
S M T W T F S	S M T W T F S	S M T W T F S
1 2 3 4	1 2	1 2 3 4 5 6
5 6 7 8 9 10 11	3 4 5 6 7 8 9	7 8 9 10 11 12 13
12 13 14 15 16 17 18	10 11 12 13 14 15 16	14 15 16 17 18 19 20
19 20 21 22 23 24 25	17 18 19 20 21 22 23	21 22 23 24 25 26 27
26 27 28 29 30	24 25 26 27 28 29 30	28 29 30
	31	

OCTOBER

For fresh, flavorful mushrooms, grow your own with a mushroom kit. Choose from button mushrooms, shiitake, oyster mushrooms, morels, and several others. Whether you prefer growing mushrooms indoors or out, you'll find tasty types that will work well in your situation. Consult a garden-supply source book or the World Wide Web to find mail-order companies that offer mushroom kits. Then get ready to have fun!

 18 Monday

☐ ☐
HIGH   LOW

19 Tuesday

☐ ☐
HIGH   LOW

 20 Wednesday

☐ ☐
HIGH   LOW

21 Thursday

☐ ☐
HIGH   LOW

Shiitake

Oyster

Button

![mushroom] **22** Friday

HIGH   LOW

![mushroom] **23** Saturday

HIGH   LOW

![mushroom] **24** Sunday   😊 *Moon of the Changing Season*

HIGH   LOW

NOTES

September						
S	M	T	W	T	F	S
				1	2	3	4
5	6	7	8	9	10	11
12	13	14	15	16	17	18
19	20	21	22	23	24	25
26	27	28	29	30		

October						
S	M	T	W	T	F	S
					1	2
3	4	5	6	7	8	9
10	11	12	13	14	15	16
17	18	19	20	21	22	23
24	25	26	27	28	29	30
31						

November						
S	M	T	W	T	F	S
	1	2	3	4	5	6
7	8	9	10	11	12	13
14	15	16	17	18	19	20
21	22	23	24	25	26	27
28	29	30				

OCTOBER

Why pay for expensive dried arrangements when you can make your own? Create a lovely arrangement by starting with globelike alliums and spiky delphiniums to define the overall shape. Then add brightly colored globe amaranths and silver honesty seedpods. Finally, fill in with airy baby's-breath and textured grasses like pennisetum. You can grow all of these plants in your garden and air-dry them for later use.

---

 25 Monday

HIGH   LOW

---

 26 Tuesday

HIGH   LOW

---

27 Wednesday

HIGH   LOW

---

28 Thursday

HIGH   LOW

---

 29 Friday

HIGH	LOW

---

 30 Saturday

HIGH	LOW

---

 31 Sunday

HIGH	LOW

• *Halloween* • *Daylight Savings Time ends at 2:00* A.M.

 NOTES

September	October	November
S M T W T F S	S M T W T F S	S M T W T F S
1 2 3 4	1 2	1 2 3 4 5 6
5 6 7 8 9 10 11	3 4 5 6 7 8 9	7 8 9 10 11 12 13
12 13 14 15 16 17 18	10 11 12 13 14 15 16	14 15 16 17 18 19 20
19 20 21 22 23 24 25	17 18 19 20 21 22 23	21 22 23 24 25 26 27
26 27 28 29 30	24 25 26 27 28 29 30	28 29 30
	31	

NOVEMBER

Attract berry-loving birds to your yard by growing tempting fruit. Birds love to sink their beaks into the orange berries of mountain ash, the fuzzy red fruit of staghorn sumac, or the red to orange berries of hawthorns and hollies. They'll also go for the whitish blue fruits of junipers and wax myrtles and the red, blue, purple, or black berries of viburnums. And of course, many birds are mulberry maniacs!

 1 Monday

HIGH LOW

• *South Taurids meteor shower visible, peaking around the 2nd or 3rd, with an average of 15 meteors per hour*

2 Tuesday

HIGH LOW

• *Election Day*

3 Wednesday

HIGH LOW

4 Thursday

HIGH LOW

5   Friday

HIGH   LOW

6   Saturday

HIGH   LOW

7   Sunday ●

HIGH   LOW

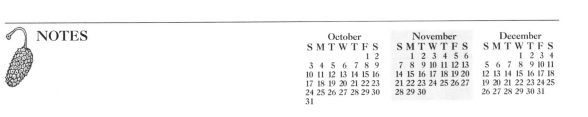

NOTES

	October								November								December					
S	M	T	W	T	F	S		S	M	T	W	T	F	S		S	M	T	W	T	F	S
					1	2			1	2	3	4	5	6					1	2	3	4
3	4	5	6	7	8	9		7	8	9	10	11	12	13		5	6	7	8	9	10	11
10	11	12	13	14	15	16		14	15	16	17	18	19	20		12	13	14	15	16	17	18
17	18	19	20	21	22	23		21	22	23	24	25	26	27		19	20	21	22	23	24	25
24	25	26	27	28	29	30		28	29	30						26	27	28	29	30	31	
31																						

NOVEMBER

Not all algae are bad. Tiny ocean algae produce
a substance called dimethylsulfoniopropionate
(DMSP), which protects them from high
salinity and freezing. Through genetic engineering,
scientists hope to transfer this production capability to agricultural
crops like citrus that are susceptible to drought, freezing, or salt
stress. By the way, DMSP is also indirectly involved in cloud
formation! Puts algae in a different light, doesn't it?

8 Monday

HIGH   LOW

9 Tuesday

HIGH   LOW

10 Wednesday

HIGH   LOW

11 Thursday

HIGH   LOW

• *Veterans Day* • *Remembrance Day (Canada)*

12 Friday

HIGH LOW

13 Saturday

HIGH LOW

14 Sunday

HIGH LOW

NOTES

NOVEMBER

If your homemade jelly doesn't jell, don't throw it out.
Give it a second chance by mixing 4 cups of the jelly juice,
½ cup water, ¼ cup sugar, 2 tablespoons lemon juice, and
4 teaspoons dry pectin. Boil the mixture for 30 seconds,
skim off the foam, then process according to your original
recipe directions.

 15 Monday

 HIGH LOW

• *Leonids meteor shower visible, peaking around the 16th or 17th, with an average of 15 meteors per hour*

 16 Tuesday ☽

HIGH LOW

---

17 Wednesday

HIGH LOW

---

18 Thursday

 HIGH LOW

19 Friday

HIGH LOW

20 Saturday

HIGH LOW

21 Sunday

HIGH LOW

NOTES

October						
S	M	T	W	T	F	S
					1	2
3	4	5	6	7	8	9
10	11	12	13	14	15	16
17	18	19	20	21	22	23
24	25	26	27	28	29	30
31						

November						
S	M	T	W	T	F	S
	1	2	3	4	5	6
7	8	9	10	11	12	13
14	15	16	17	18	19	20
21	22	23	24	25	26	27
28	29	30				

December						
S	M	T	W	T	F	S
			1	2	3	4
5	6	7	8	9	10	11
12	13	14	15	16	17	18
19	20	21	22	23	24	25
26	27	28	29	30	31	

NOVEMBER

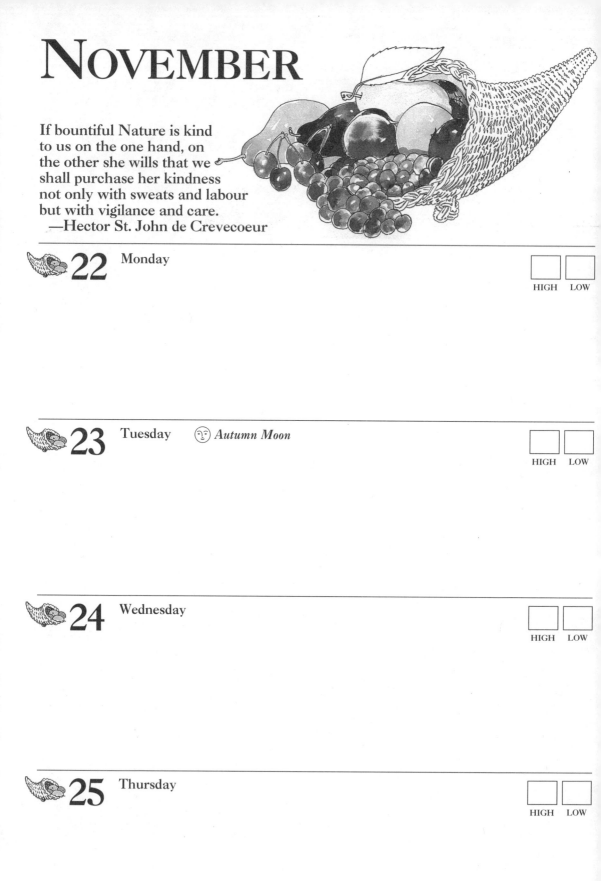

If bountiful Nature is kind
to us on the one hand, on
the other she wills that we
shall purchase her kindness
not only with sweats and labour
but with vigilance and care.
   —Hector St. John de Crevecoeur

---

22 Monday

HIGH LOW

---

23 Tuesday   🌙 *Autumn Moon*

HIGH LOW

---

24 Wednesday

HIGH LOW

---

25 Thursday

HIGH LOW

• *Thanksgiving*

 **26** Friday

HIGH   LOW

 27 Saturday

HIGH   LOW

 28 Sunday

HIGH   LOW

 NOTES

October	November	December
S M T W T F S	S M T W T F S	S M T W T F S
1 2	1 2 3 4 5 6	1 2 3 4
3 4 5 6 7 8 9	7 8 9 10 11 12 13	5 6 7 8 9 10 11
10 11 12 13 14 15 16	14 15 16 17 18 19 20	12 13 14 15 16 17 18
17 18 19 20 21 22 23	21 22 23 24 25 26 27	19 20 21 22 23 24 25
24 25 26 27 28 29 30	28 29 30	26 27 28 29 30 31
31		

NOVEMBER • DECEMBER

The Christmas cactus isn't fussy about room for its roots. But even though it likes potbound conditions, it still needs repotting every year or so. The best time to repot is in spring, when new growth appears. Select a pot that's only slightly larger than the one the cactus is in. Use a light mix of soil, sand, peat moss, and compost to provide good drainage—a must for this tropical epiphyte.

 29 Monday

HIGH LOW

 30 Tuesday

HIGH LOW

1 Wednesday

HIGH LOW

2 Thursday

HIGH LOW

3
Friday

HIGH LOW

• Hanukkah begins at sundown

4
Saturday

HIGH LOW

5
Sunday

HIGH LOW

NOTES

October						
S	M	T	W	T	F	S
					1	2
3	4	5	6	7	8	9
10	11	12	13	14	15	16
17	18	19	20	21	22	23
24	25	26	27	28	29	30
31						

November						
S	M	T	W	T	F	S
	1	2	3	4	5	6
7	8	9	10	11	12	13
14	15	16	17	18	19	20
21	22	23	24	25	26	27
28	29	30				

December						
S	M	T	W	T	F	S
			1	2	3	4
5	6	7	8	9	10	11
12	13	14	15	16	17	18
19	20	21	22	23	24	25
26	27	28	29	30	31	

DECEMBER

"Neoprene socks make a great gardener's gift," says
Delilah Smittle of Allentown, Pennsylvania. "They're
made from the same material as the wet suits that divers
wear, so they're not only waterproof but will also keep
your feet warm, too! With a pair of these waterproof
socks, I can wear my leakiest, most comfy old sneakers
to garden in and still keep my feet snug and dry."
Neoprene socks are sold through mail-order sportswear
catalogs and at shops that sell fishing supplies.

---

 6 Monday

HIGH LOW

---

 7 Tuesday ●

HIGH LOW

---

 8 Wednesday

HIGH LOW

---

9 Thursday

HIGH LOW

---

 10 Friday

HIGH   LOW

---

11 Saturday

HIGH   LOW

---

12 Sunday

HIGH   LOW

• *Geminids meteor shower visible, peaking around the 13th or 14th, with an average of 50 meteors per hour*

 **NOTES**

November	December	January
S M T W T F S	S M T W T F S	S M T W T F S
1 2 3 4 5 6	1 2 3 4	1
7 8 9 10 11 12 13	5 6 7 8 9 10 11	2 3 4 5 6 7 8
14 15 16 17 18 19 20	12 13 14 15 16 17 18	9 10 11 12 13 14 15
21 22 23 24 25 26 27	19 20 21 22 23 24 25	16 17 18 19 20 21 22
28 29 30	26 27 28 29 30 31	23 24 25 26 27 28 29
		30 31

DECEMBER

"Winter is a wonderful time to see who's visiting your yard—or coming even closer to the house," says Ellen Phillips, managing editor of Rodale Garden and Nature Books. "I love to see the bird, squirrel, and cat tracks crossing the fresh snow on my back deck." But don't despair if this winter is snowless. According to Ellen, mud is just as good. "I can find animal tracks in my yard all year. My favorites are the raccoon tracks in my muddy creek bottom."

13 Monday

HIGH   LOW

14 Tuesday

HIGH   LOW

15 Wednesday

HIGH   LOW

16 Thursday

HIGH   LOW

Bird Rabbit Cat Squirrel Raccoon

17 Friday

HIGH LOW

18 Saturday

HIGH LOW

19 Sunday

HIGH LOW

NOTES

<table>
<tr><th colspan="7">November</th><th colspan="7">December</th><th colspan="7">January</th></tr>
<tr><td>S</td><td>M</td><td>T</td><td>W</td><td>T</td><td>F</td><td>S</td><td>S</td><td>M</td><td>T</td><td>W</td><td>T</td><td>F</td><td>S</td><td>S</td><td>M</td><td>T</td><td>W</td><td>T</td><td>F</td><td>S</td></tr>
<tr><td></td><td>1</td><td>2</td><td>3</td><td>4</td><td>5</td><td>6</td><td></td><td></td><td></td><td>1</td><td>2</td><td>3</td><td>4</td><td></td><td></td><td></td><td></td><td></td><td></td><td>1</td></tr>
<tr><td>7</td><td>8</td><td>9</td><td>10</td><td>11</td><td>12</td><td>13</td><td>5</td><td>6</td><td>7</td><td>8</td><td>9</td><td>10</td><td>11</td><td>2</td><td>3</td><td>4</td><td>5</td><td>6</td><td>7</td><td>8</td></tr>
<tr><td>14</td><td>15</td><td>16</td><td>17</td><td>18</td><td>19</td><td>20</td><td>12</td><td>13</td><td>14</td><td>15</td><td>16</td><td>17</td><td>18</td><td>9</td><td>10</td><td>11</td><td>12</td><td>13</td><td>14</td><td>15</td></tr>
<tr><td>21</td><td>22</td><td>23</td><td>24</td><td>25</td><td>26</td><td>27</td><td>19</td><td>20</td><td>21</td><td>22</td><td>23</td><td>24</td><td>25</td><td>16</td><td>17</td><td>18</td><td>19</td><td>20</td><td>21</td><td>22</td></tr>
<tr><td>28</td><td>29</td><td>30</td><td></td><td></td><td></td><td></td><td>26</td><td>27</td><td>28</td><td>29</td><td>30</td><td>31</td><td></td><td>23</td><td>24</td><td>25</td><td>26</td><td>27</td><td>28</td><td>29</td></tr>
<tr><td></td><td></td><td></td><td></td><td></td><td></td><td></td><td></td><td></td><td></td><td></td><td></td><td></td><td></td><td>30</td><td>31</td><td></td><td></td><td></td><td></td><td></td></tr>
</table>

DECEMBER

Let us have peas.
—Charles Dudley Warner

---

 20 Monday

□ □
HIGH LOW

---

 21 Tuesday

□ □
HIGH LOW

---

 22 Wednesday 😊 *Winter Moon*

□ □
HIGH LOW

• *Winter begins at 2:44 A.M.*

---

 23 Thursday

HIGH LOW

 24 Friday

HIGH   LOW

 25 Saturday

HIGH   LOW

• *Christmas*

 26 Sunday

HIGH   LOW

 NOTES

November						
S	M	T	W	T	F	S
	1	2	3	4	5	6
7	8	9	10	11	12	13
14	15	16	17	18	19	20
21	22	23	24	25	26	27
28	29	30				

December						
S	M	T	W	T	F	S
			1	2	3	4
5	6	7	8	9	10	11
12	13	14	15	16	17	18
19	20	21	22	23	24	25
26	27	28	29	30	31	

January						
S	M	T	W	T	F	S
						1
2	3	4	5	6	7	8
9	10	11	12	13	14	15
16	17	18	19	20	21	22
23	24	25	26	27	28	29
30	31					

DECEMBER · JANUARY

We anticipate with joy what each season will bring,
Be it frost or thaw or birds that sing,
Snow-capped evergreens, fields of flowers,
Geese flying high, fruited bowers,
Orchards will bloom, birds will nest.
Through the evolution of seasons, Earth is blessed.
—Edna Frohock

---

 27 Monday

HIGH	LOW

---

 28 Tuesday

HIGH	LOW

---

 29 Wednesday

HIGH	LOW

---

 30 Thursday

HIGH	LOW

 31 Friday

| HIGH | LOW |

 1 Saturday

| HIGH | LOW |

• *New Year's Day*

 2 Sunday

| HIGH | LOW |

 NOTES

November	December	January
S M T W T F S	S M T W T F S	S M T W T F S
1 2 3 4 5 6	1 2 3 4	1
7 8 9 10 11 12 13	5 6 7 8 9 10 11	2 3 4 5 6 7 8
14 15 16 17 18 19 20	12 13 14 15 16 17 18	9 10 11 12 13 14 15
21 22 23 24 25 26 27	19 20 21 22 23 24 25	16 17 18 19 20 21 22
28 29 30	26 27 28 29 30 31	23 24 25 26 27 28 29
		30 31

GARDEN ACTIVITY SCHEDULE

LAST SPRING FROST _____   FIRST FALL FROST _____

THINGS TO DO IN THE GARDEN	TO BE DONE BY (DATE)

Designing Your Garden

If you make a garden plan first, chances are your garden will be more productive and satisfying, and you'll save money by buying only the number of plants you have room for.

To help you plan your garden, turn the page and refer to the Garden Plotter. You may want to make several photocopies of these pages so you can try out different designs before settling on the one that's just right.

The first step in drawing a plan is to determine your scale. You'll want to select a scale that allows you to include the most details but still allows you to fit the whole garden onto the Garden Plotter. See the sample 10 × 18-foot vegetable garden below. Note the scale of this plan: Each square on the paper represents 1 foot in the garden. If you have a large garden, you may want to make each square equal 2 feet. For small gardens, you can make each square equal 6 inches. Do whatever works best for your garden space.

After you determine your scale, think about where each plant should go. Ask yourself questions, such as: What patterns do I want to create? Is my garden formal or informal? How tall will each plant grow? Will the taller plants block out sunlight for shorter plants, or will they provide needed shade? Will early-season plants make way for later-season plants? What vegetables should grow near each other? (Turn to "Companions, Allies, and Enemies in Your Garden" for help in deciding which plants to pair up.)

After you make these important decisions, you're ready to draw. I always use a pencil in case I change my mind during the process. Using your chosen scale, mark the placement of plants within the garden space. (Refer to the planting and spacing guides in this calendar for the spacing requirements of several common garden plants.) Be sure to allow enough space for the mature size of each plant. You may wish to use different symbols, such as Xs and Os, to represent different types of plants, or just outline the areas where groups of plants, such as carrots or lettuce, will grow. Label each planting, or create a key as I did in the plan below, so you remember later what your abbreviations and symbols mean.

Voilà! That's all there is to it. Once your garden plot plan is finished, you're all set to get your seeds and plants and head out to your garden.

Heidi's 10' x 18' Vegetable Garden

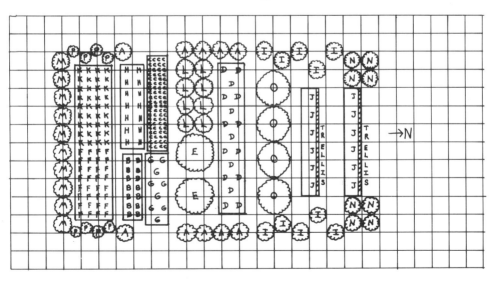

Scale:
1 square = 1 foot

A = globe amaranth
B = basil
C = carrot
D = Swiss chard
E = tomato
F = garlic

G = German chamomile
H = lettuce
I = marigold
J = pole bean
K = onion

L = pepper
M = snapdragon
N = nasturtium
O = medium-sized sunflower
P = parsley

GARDEN PLOTTER

GARDEN PLOTTER

GARDEN PLOTTER

Vegetable Planting and Spacing Guide

Vegetable	Seed Planting Depth	Intensive Spacing (Distance between plants in all directions)	Conventional Spacing (Distance between plants in row)	(Distance between rows)
Asparagus (crowns)	6–10	—	24	36–48
Beans, snap bush	1	4–6	2–4	18–36
Beets	½	2–6	2–4	12–30
Broccoli	¼	15–18	12–24	18–36
Brussels sprouts	½	18	18–24	30–36
Cabbage	¼	15–18	12–24	24–36
Carrots	¼	2–3	1–3	16–30
Cauliflower	½	18	24	36
Chard	½	9	9	18
Collards	½	15	15	36
Corn	1	18	8–12	30–42
Cucumbers	½–1	12–18	3–6	14–42
Eggplants	¼	24	24	24–36
Lettuce, leaf	¼	6–9	8–12	12–24
Melons	½	36	36–96	72–96
Okra	½	18	10–14	24–48
Onions (sets)	1	4–6	1–4	16–24
Peas	1	2–6	1–3	24–48
Peppers	½	12–15	12–24	18–36
Potatoes	4	10–12	6–12	30–42
Radishes	¼	2–3	½–1	8–18
Spinach	¼	4–6	2–6	12–36
Squash, summer and winter	½–1	24–36	39–96	72–96
Tomatoes (staked)	¼–½	18–24	12–24	36–48

Note: All distances given in inches.

FLOWER PLANTING
AND SPACING GUIDE

FLOWER	LIGHT	SOIL	SPACING BETWEEN TRANSPLANTS (IN INCHES)
ANNUALS			
Ageratum	Full sun to part shade	Wide range	6–12
Alyssum, sweet	Full sun to part shade	Average, well-drained	6–8
Cleome	Full sun to part shade	Average, well-drained	12–24
Coleus	Part shade to full shade	Moist, rich, well-drained	Small: 6–10 Tall: 12–20
Geranium, zonal	Full sun; part shade for variegated types	Moist, rich, well-drained	12–18
Impatiens (*I. wallerana*)	Full shade	Moist, rich	12
Marigold	Full sun	Average, well-drained	Dwarf: 6–8 Medium: 12–15 Tall: 18–24
Nasturtium	Full sun	Poor to average	Bush: 8–12 Vine: 24–36
Petunia	Full sun	Moist, well-drained	8–12
Snapdragon	Full sun to part shade	Rich, light, well-drained	Dwarf: 6–8 Medium: 9–10 Tall: 12–18
Sunflower	Full sun	Average, well-drained	Small: 12 Tall: 24–36
Zinnia	Full sun	Average, well-drained	Dwarf: 6–9 Medium: 10–12 Tall: 18–24
PERENNIALS			
Aster	Full sun	Rich, moist, well-drained	Small: 9–12 Tall: 24–36
Astilbe	Part shade	Rich, moist, well-drained	Small: 10–15 Tall: 20–36
Bee balm	Full sun to part shade	Moist, average, well-drained	12–24
Black-eyed Susan	Full sun	Tolerates wide range of soils	Small: 12–18 Tall: 24–36
Chrysanthemum	Full sun	Rich, moist, well-drained	Small: 12–15 Tall: 18–24
Coreopsis	Full sun	Tolerates wide range of soils; well-drained	Small: 6–10 Tall: 12–18
Daylily	Full sun to part shade	Tolerates wide range of soils	12–24
Delphinium	Full sun to part shade	Rich, moist, well-drained, slightly acid to alkaline	Small: 12–18 Tall: 24–36
Dianthus	Full sun to part shade, depending on species	Rich, light, well-drained	Small: 6–9 Tall: 10–18
Hosta	Part shade to full shade	Rich, moist, well-drained	Small: 10–12 Medium: 18–24 Tall: 36–48
Iris, bearded	Full sun to part shade	Rich, moist, well-drained	12–24
Phlox	Full sun to part shade, depending on species	Rich to average, moist, well-drained, depending on species	Small: 6–8 Medium:10–18 Tall: 24–36
Poppy	Full sun; part shade in warm climates	Average to rich, well-drained	Small: 6–12 Tall: 18–36
Yarrow	Full sun	Average to poor, well-drained	12–36

GERMINATING AND TRANSPLANTING KEY FOR POPULAR VEGETABLES

Vegetable	Best Soil Temperature (°F) for Germination	Average Days to Germination	Weeks to Transplant Size (from sowing)	Spring Setting-Out Dates (relative to frost-free date)		Comments
				Weeks Before	Weeks After*	
Beans, snap	75–80	7	3–4	—	8	Treat roots gently when transplanting.
Beets	75	7–14	4	4	—	Disturb roots as little as possible.
Broccoli	60–75	5–10	6–8	4	2–3	Transplants well.
Brussels sprouts	68–75	5–10	6–8	4	2–3	Transplant well.
Cabbage	68–75	5–10	6–8	5	2–3	Direct-seed mid- and late-season varieties.
Cauliflower	68–86	5–10	6–8	4	2	Direct-seed fall and winter crops.
Cucumbers	70–86	7–10	4	—	8	Often direct-seeded; transplants shorten time to harvest.
Eggplants	70–86	10	6–8	—	2–3	Transplant well.
Lettuce (all kinds)	68–70	7–10	4–6	2	3	Direct-seed some, too, to stagger harvest.
Melons	80–86	4–10	4	—	2–3	Often direct-seeded; transplants shorten time to harvest.
Onions (from seed)	68–70	10–14	4–6	6	2	Plant onion sets at same time seedlings are set out.
Peppers	75–85	10	6–8	—	2–3	Transplant well.
Squash, summer	70–95	7–10	4	—	4	Often direct-seeded; transplants shorten time to harvest.
Squash, winter	70–95	7–10	4	—	3–4	Often direct-seeded; transplants shorten time to harvest.
Swiss chard	50–85	7–10	4	3–6	—	Disturb roots as little as possible.
Tomatoes	75–80	7–14	6–10	—	4	Can plant earlier with protection.

*Indicates latest commonly observed setting-out date. With adequate protection from heat, insect pests, drought, and such, the dates may be extended.

DIRECT SEEDING DATES

This table can serve as a general timetable to help you schedule plantings out in the garden. But first, call your local extension agent to find out the frost-free date in your area. Use this date as your point of reference as you add or subtract weeks, depending on the hardiness of the crops you're planting. *Hardy* plants can withstand subfreezing temperatures. *Half-hardy* plants can withstand only some light freezing. The fruit and leaves of *tender* crops are injured by light frost, while *very tender* plants need warm temperatures (above 70° F) to grow. Any exposure to temperatures just above freezing will damage fruit and leaves.

FROST-FREE DATE _____

COOL-SEASON CROPS		WARM-SEASON CROPS	
HARDY: PLANT 4–6 WEEKS BEFORE FROST-FREE DATE	**HALF-HARDY:** PLANT 2–4 WEEKS BEFORE FROST-FREE DATE	**TENDER:** PLANT ON FROST-FREE DATE	**VERY TENDER:** PLANT 1 WEEK OR MORE AFTER FROST-FREE DATE
Asparagus	Beets	Beans, snap	Corn (depending
Broccoli	Carrots*	Corn (depending	on variety)
Brussels sprouts	Cauliflower	on variety)	Cucumbers
Cabbage	Lettuce*	Okra	Eggplants
Collards	Potatoes	Tomatoes	Melons
Onions	Radishes*		Peppers
Peas	Swiss chard		Squash, summer
Spinach			Squash, winter

*These particular half-hardy plants can be planted outdoors at the same time as hardy crops if they are protected from extreme cold.

HOW TO FIGURE THE LAST PLANTING DATE

VEGETABLE	DAYS TO MATURITY[1] +	DAYS TO GERMI- NATION[2] +	DAYS TO TRANS- PLANTING +	2 WEEKS SHORT-DAY FACTOR[3] +	BEFORE FIRST FROST[4] =	DAYS TO COUNT BACK FROM FIRST FROST DATE
TENDER						
Beans, snap	50	7	direct seed	14	14	85
Corn	65	4	direct seed	14	14	97
Cucumbers	55	3	direct seed	14	14	86
Squash, summer	50	3	direct seed	14	14	81
Tomatoes	55	6	21	14	14	110
LIGHT FROST						
Beets	55	5	direct seed	14	—	74
Cauliflower	50	5	21	14	—	90
Lettuce, head	65	3	14	14	—	96
Lettuce, leaf	45	3	14	14	—	76
Peas	50	6	direct seed	14	—	70
HEAVY FROST						
Broccoli	55	5	21	14	—	95
Brussels sprouts	80	5	21	14	—	120
Cabbage	60	4	21	14	—	99
Carrots	65	6	direct seed	14	—	85
Collards	55	4	21	14	—	94
Radishes	25	3	direct seed	14	—	42
Spinach	45	5	direct seed	14	—	64
Swiss chard	50	5	direct seed	14	—	69

[1] These figures are for the fastest-maturing varieties we could find. Fast-maturing cultivars are best for fall crops. But for the variety you have, get the correct number of days from your seed catalog.

[2] These figures for days to germination assume a soil temperature of 80°F.

[3] The short-day factor is necessary because the time to maturity in seed catalogs always assumes the long days and warm temperatures of early summer. Crops always take longer in late summer and fall.

[4] Frost-tender vegetables must mature at least two weeks before frost if they are to produce a substantial harvest.

GERMINATING AND TRANSPLANTING KEY FOR POPULAR FLOWERS

	FLOWER	WEEKS BEFORE LAST FROST TO START SEEDS INDOORS	BEST SOIL TEMPERATURE (°F) FOR GERMINATION	SEED PLANTING DEPTH (IN INCHES)	AVERAGE DAYS TO GERMINATION	COMMENTS
ANNUALS	Ageratum	6–8	70–80	Surface	5–10	Set plants out or direct-se after last frost.
	Ayssum, sweet	6–8	60–75	Surface	8–15	Set plants out around las frost. Or, direct-seed 2– weeks before last frost. Often self-sows.
	Cleome	4–6	Prechill seeds in refrigerator 1–2 weeks; then 70–85.	Surface	10–14	Set plants out or direct-se just after last frost. Ofte self-sows.
	Coleus	8–10	70–75	Surface; place pot in plastic bag until seedlings appear.	10–12	Tender perennials grown annuals. Set plants out after last frost.
	Impatiens (I. wallerana)	8–10	70–80	Surface; place pot in plastic bag until seedlings appear.	7–20	Set plants out 1–2 weeks after last frost. Suscepti to soilborne diseases; us sterile equipment.
	Marigold	6–8. Start triploids and African marigolds indoors.	70–75	⅛–¼	5–7	Set plants out after last fro Start French and signet marigolds indoors or direct-seed after last frost
	Nasturtium	4–6. Does not transplant well; use peat pots.	65	¼	7–12	Set plants out after last frost. Or, direct-seed 1–2 weeks before last frost.
	Petunia	8–10	70–80	Surface; place pot in plastic bag until seedlings appear.	7–20	Set plants out after last frost.
	Snapdragon	6–8	70–75	Surface	10–20	Set plants out after last frost. In cool climates, direct-seed a few weeks before last frost.
	Sunflower	4–6	70–85	½	5–14	Set plants out or direct-se after last frost.
	Zinnia	4–6. Does not transplant well; use peat pots.	70–80	¼	5–7	In warm climates, direct-seed after danger of frost has passed.

	WEEKS BEFORE LAST FROST TO START SEEDS INDOORS	BEST SOIL TEMPERATURE (°F) FOR GERMINATION	SEED PLANTING DEPTH (IN INCHES)	AVERAGE DAYS TO GERMINATION	COMMENTS
FLOWER					
Aster	8–10	Prechill seeds in refrigerator for 2 weeks; then 70–75.	⅛; place pot in plastic bag until seedlings appear.	14–36	Set plants out after last frost. Or, direct-seed in early spring or late fall.
Astilbe	6–8	60-70	Surface	14-28	Set plants out after last frost. Or, direct-seed in early spring or fall.
Bee balm	4-8	60–70	⅛	14-21	Set plants out about 1 week before last frost. Or, direct-seed 2–4 weeks before last frost.
Black-eyed Susan	6–8	70–75. Prechill seeds of *R. fulgida* 2 weeks before sowing.	⅛	7–21	Set plants out after last frost, or direct-seed 2 weeks before last frost.
Chrysanthemum	6–10 before planting out.	60–70	Surface	7–28	Set plants out after last frost. Or, direct-seed in spring or summer.
Coreopsis	6–10	55–70	Surface	14–25	Set plants out after last frost. Or, direct-seed in spring or summer.
Daylily	8–10 before planting out.	Refrigerate in moist growing medium in plastic bag for 6 weeks; then 60–70.	⅛	21–49	Set plants out after last frost. Or, direct-seed in late fall or early spring. Takes 2–3 years from seed to bloom.
Delphinium	8–10	Prechill seeds in refrigerator for 1 week. Thereafter, many species prefer 65–75.	¼	7-21	Set plants out after last frost. Or, direct-seed in summer for flowers next year.
Dianthus	4	60–70	⅛	14–21	Set plants out or direct-seed in early spring.
Poppy	6–10. Does not transplant well; use peat pots.	55	⅛ (most species); surface sow *P. orientale.*	10–20	Set plants out after last frost. Or, direct-seed in late fall or early spring.
Yarrow	8–10 before planting out.	60–70	Surface	10–15	Set plants out or direct-seed in early spring.

PERENNIALS

PLANTING
SCHEDULE

For a head start on the gardening season, here's a worksheet to aid your planning. As you refer to seed starting and transplanting charts included in this calendar, jot down the planting dates for the flowers and vegetables you'll be growing. This would also be a good place to figure out the timing for any succession planting you'll be doing. Use the Notes column as a place to write down any special planting instructions. Throughout the season, just flip back to this page for a handy reminder of what you should be planting as areas of the garden open up.

DATE TO PLANT	PLANT	NOTES

ADDITIONAL NOTES

COMPANIONS, ALLIES, AND ENEMIES IN YOUR GARDEN

Through the years gardeners have observed that some plants grow well together, while others do not. This chart presents traditional companions (plants that have compatible growth habits and share space well), allies (plants that enhance growth and ward off insects), and enemies (plants that deter good growth). As you plan your garden, try some of the beneficial pairings given below and see if they bring you good results.

ASPARAGUS: *Companions:* Basil, parsley, tomatoes. *Ally:* Pot marigolds deter beetles. *Enemy:* Onions.

BEANS: *Companions:* Beets (to bush beans only), cabbage family, carrots, celery, corn, cucumbers, eggplants, peas, potatoes, radishes, strawberries, Swiss chard. *Allies:* Marigolds deter Mexican bean beetles and nematodes; nasturtiums and rosemary deter bean beetles; summer savory deters bean beetles, improves growth and flavor. *Enemies:* Garlic, onions, and shallots stunt the growth of beans.

BEETS: *Companions:* Bush beans, cabbage family, lettuce, onions. *Ally:* Garlic improves growth and flavor. *Enemy:* Pole beans and beets stunt each other's growth.

CABBAGE FAMILY (broccoli, brussels sprouts, cabbage, cauliflower, Chinese cabbage, kale, and kohlrabi): *Companions:* Beans, beets, celery, cucumbers, lettuce, onions, potatoes, spinach, Swiss chard. *Allies:* Chamomile and garlic improve growth and flavor; catnip, hyssop, rosemary, and sage deter cabbage moths; dill improves growth and vigor; mint deters cabbage moths and ants, improves vigor and flavor; nasturtiums deter beetles and aphids; southernwood deters cabbage moths, improves growth and flavor; tansy deters cabbageworms and cutworms. *Enemies:* Pole beans and strawberries; tomatoes and kohlrabi stunt each other's growth.

CARROTS: *Companions:* Beans, lettuce, onions, peas, peppers, radishes, tomatoes. *Allies:* Chives improve growth and flavor; rosemary and sage deter carrot flies. *Enemy:* Dill retards growth.

CELERY: *Companions:* Beans, cabbage family, squash, tomatoes. *Allies:* Chives, garlic, and nasturtiums deter aphids. *Enemies:* Carrots, parsnips.

CORN: *Companions:* Beans, cucumbers, melons, parsley, peas, potatoes, pumpkins, squash. *Allies:* Odorless marigolds and white geraniums deter Japanese beetles; pigweed raises nutrients from the subsoil to where the corn can reach them. *Enemy:* Tomatoes and corn are attacked by the same worm.

CUCUMBERS: *Companions:* Beans, cabbage family, corn, peas, radishes, tomatoes. *Allies:* Marigolds deter beetles; nasturtiums deter aphids and beetles, improve growth and flavor; oregano deters pests in general; tansy deters ants, beetles, and flying insects. *Enemy:* Sage is generally injurious to cucumbers.

EGGPLANTS: *Companions:* Beans, peppers, potatoes. *Ally:* Marigolds deter nematodes.

LETTUCE: *Companions:* Beets, cabbage family, carrots, onions, radishes, strawberries. *Allies:* Chives and garlic deter aphids.

PARSLEY: *Companions:* Asparagus, corn, tomatoes.

PEAS: *Companions:* Beans, carrots, corn, cucumbers, potatoes, radishes, turnips. *Allies:* Chives deter aphids; mint improves vigor and flavor. *Enemies:* Garlic and onions stunt the growth of peas.

PEPPERS: *Companions:* Carrots, eggplants, onions, tomatoes.

POTATOES: *Companions:* Beans, cabbage family, corn, eggplants, peas. *Allies:* Horseradish, planted at the corners of the potato patch, provides general protection; marigolds deter beetles. *Enemy:* Tomatoes and potatoes are attacked by the same blight.

PUMPKINS: *Companions:* Corn, melons, squash. *Allies:* Marigolds and nasturtiums deter beetles; oregano provides general pest protection. *Enemy:* Potatoes.

RADISHES: *Companions:* Beans, carrots, cucumbers, lettuce, melons, peas. *Allies:* Chervil and nasturtiums improve growth and flavor. *Enemy:* Hyssop.

SPINACH: *Companions:* Cabbage family, strawberries.

SQUASH: *Companions:* Celery, corn, melons, pumpkins. *Allies:* Borage deters worms, improves growth and flavor; marigolds deter beetles; nasturtiums deter squash bugs and beetles; oregano provides general pest protection. *Enemy:* Potatoes.

STRAWBERRIES: *Companions:* Beans, lettuce, onions, spinach, thyme. *Allies:* Borage strengthens resistance to insects and disease; thyme, as a border, deters worms. *Enemy:* Cabbage.

SWISS CHARD: *Companions:* Beans, cabbage family, onions.

TOMATOES: *Companions:* Asparagus, carrots, celery, cucumbers, onions, parsley, peppers. *Allies:* Basil repels flies and mosquitoes, improves growth and flavor; bee balm, chives, and mint improve health and flavor; dill, until mature, improves growth and vigor; once mature, it stunts tomato growth; marigolds deter nematodes; pot marigolds deter tomato worms and general garden pests. *Enemies:* Corn and tomatoes are attacked by the same worm; mature dill retards tomato growth; kohlrabi stunts tomato growth; potatoes and tomatoes are attacked by the same blight.

TURNIPS: *Companion:* Peas. *Enemy:* Potatoes.

Pest Identification and Control

Insect	Description	Host	Damage	Control
Aphids	Soft bodied, ⅛", pear-shaped insects	Most plants	Adults and nymphs suck plant juices, causing distorted, curled foliage.	Wash off with water. Beneficials.
Borer, squash vine	White larva with brown head; adult is narrow-winged moth with red abdomen	Squash, pumpkins, melons, gourds	Larvae bore into stem base, causing plant to wilt or die.	Row covers for young plants. Slit infested stems and remove borers; bury slit in soil.
Cabbage looper	Green 1½" larva with white stripes; looping motion when moving	Cabbage family	Larvae chew large holes in leaves.	Handpick. Beneficials. BTK sprays.
Cabbageworm, imported	Green 1¼" larva; adult is white butterfly with black tip and 2–3 spots	Cabbage family	Larvae chew large holes in leaves, leaving green droppings.	Row covers. BTK sprays.
Cucumber beetles, spotted or striped	Yellowish ¼" beetles with black spots or stripes; larvae are white grubs	Squash, corn, cucumbers, and other crops	Adults feed on various vegetables. Larvae feed on roots of corn (spotted) or squash(striped), stunting or killing plants. Both stages can transmit viruses.	Row covers. Resistant varieties.
Cutworms	Fat brown-gray 1"–2" caterpillars	Young seedlings	Larvae sever plant stems near soil line.	Paper or cardboard collars around transplants.
Flea beetles	Tiny, shiny black, brown, or bronze ⅒" beetles	Vegetables, especially eggplant, and flowers	Beetles chew many tiny holes in leaves.	Row covers.
Japanese beetle	Adult is blue-green and bronze ½" beetle; larva is a fat, white grub.	Wide range of plants	Adults skeletonize leaves and flowers. Larvae feed on roots of lawn and garden plants.	Handpick. Apply milky spore disease to soil.
Mexican bean beetle	Oval yellow-orange beetle with 16 black spots; larva is bright yellow, 5/16", with large spines.	Beans	Adults and larvae skeletonize leaves, feeding on leaf undersides.	Row covers. Handpick. Beneficials.
Scales	Adults are hard or soft ⅒"–⅕" round to oval bumps.	Trees, shrubs, fruits, houseplants	All stages suck plant juices and weaken plant.	Beneficials. Superior oil spray.
Slugs and snails	Soft-bodied gray to brown mollusks; snails have shells, slugs don't.	Wide range of plants	Slugs and snails chew large holes in leaves, stems and bulbs.	Drown them in shallow pans of beer. Copper strip barriers. Diatomaceous earth.
Squash bug	Adult is oval, ⅝", brownish black bug; nymphs are gray or whitish green.	Cucurbits	Nymphs and adults suck plant juices, causing leaves and shoots to blacken.	Resistant varieties. Row covers. Handpick.

VEGETABLE, FLOWER, AND HERB LOG

PLANT NAME	DATE PLANTED	NOTES

VEGETABLE, FLOWER, AND HERB LOG

PLANT NAME	DATE PLANTED	NOTES

VEGETABLE, FLOWER, AND HERB LOG

PLANT NAME	DATE PLANTED	NOTES

VEGETABLE, FLOWER, AND HERB LOG

PLANT NAME	DATE PLANTED	NOTES

VEGETABLE, FLOWER, AND HERB LOG

PLANT NAME	DATE PLANTED	NOTES

Vegetable, Flower, and Herb Log

Plant Name	Date Planted	Notes

FRUIT AND BERRY LOG

PLANT NAME	DATE PLANTED	DATE PRUNED	HARVEST START	FINISH	PERFORMANCE

FRUIT AND BERRY LOG

PLANT NAME	DATE PLANTED	DATE PRUNED	HARVEST START	HARVEST FINISH	PERFORMANCE

SEED INVENTORY

This worksheet will help you keep track of the odds and ends of vegetable, herb, and flower seeds you have on hand. If you store the leftovers from one season's planting in a cool, dry place, most seeds will remain usable for up to 3 years. Remember to test stored seeds before planting to make sure they'll still germinate.

SEED	DATE PURCHASED	AMOUNT PURCHASED	SEED SOURCE	AMOUNT LEFT AFTER SOWING	TO BE USED BY	AMOUNT TO REORDER

Seed Inventory

Seed	Date Purchased	Amount Purchased	Seed Source	Amount Left after Sowing	To Be Used By	Amount to Reorder

HARVEST GUIDE

After all the time and energy you've put into your garden, you deserve the freshest, best-tasting harvest possible. That means you must watch carefully for signs that your vegetables and fruits have reached their peak. Read the following clues for prime-time harvesting.

APPLES: Look for full-size fruit with good color that separates easily from the tree. A taste test is the best indicator.

BEANS, SNAP: The best beans are young and thin with no bulging seeds inside the pods.

BEETS: Take a few greens through the season to add life to salads. Don't let the roots grow too big: 1½ to 2 inches in diameter is big enough. The larger the beet, the woodier, and the more likely it is to crack.

BLUEBERRIES: Berries ripen over a 2- to 5-week period. The color is deceptive since berries turn deep blue before they're ripe. Taste a few before harvesting in earnest.

BROCCOLI: Dark green is the color you want. Any signs of yellow mean you've waited too long.

BRUSSELS SPROUTS: Sprouts are ready once they become firm. The ones at the bottom mature first. Don't let sprouts get bigger than 1 inch. A few light frosts will enhance their flavor.

CABBAGE: Take them as you need them once heads have formed. Left too long in the garden they split but will still be usable.

CARROTS: Enjoy pencil-size thinnings through the season. Don't let carrots grow fatter than 1½ inches across; otherwise they'll become woody.

CAULIFLOWER: Don't expect giant, supermarket-size heads. Pick when they're firm, smooth, and about 6 inches around. Yellow or loose mealy curds indicate that you've delayed the harvest too long.

CHERRIES: Ripe sweet cherries pull off the tree easily, stem and all. Taste is the surest guide. Sour cherries are ready when they come off easily, leaving pits attached to stems.

CORN: Watch for dark, dry silks, then feel for plump kernels. Pierce a kernel with a fingernail; clear liquid means wait a few days, milky liquid means it's time to put the water on, and pasty liquid means the corn is suitable for canning but past its prime for fresh eating.

CUCUMBERS: Start picking once they're 3 inches long. Over-the-hill cucumbers are yellow with tough skins and large seeds.

EGGPLANTS: The smaller and glossier, the better. Older, larger eggplants are bitter with tough skins.

GRAPES: Look for grapes that have full color and feel soft.

LETTUCE: The younger they are, the sweeter and more tender they'll be. Harvest a few outer leaves at a time from leaf lettuces. Head lettuces are ready when the center starts to feel firm. Pick loosehead lettuces when the heads begin to form.

MELONS: A muskmelon (cantaloupe) or watermelon will separate or slip from the stem when it's ready. Harvest honeydews when they turn creamy yellow and the blossom ends give just slightly under thumb pressure.

ONIONS: Take these as you need them, to use the small bulbs or green tops. For storage onions, wait to dig until the tops have dried and fallen over.

PEACHES: Watch for flattened sides to become rounded and for the background color to change from green to cream. Ripe peaches feel soft and taste unmistakably sweet.

PEARS: Pick most types when full-size but still green and firm. Put mature pears in cold storage until you are ready for them. To ripen, set them in a cool room. However, let 'Seckel' and Asian pears ripen on the tree.

PEAS: Pick when the peas begin to bulge in the pod but before they crowd each other. Snap peas are the exception—they get better as the edible pods and peas get bigger. Pick snow peas before the peas inside begin to form.

PEPPERS: Pick as soon as they're firm and green. For stuffing, let them grow to a good size. Fully mature green peppers turn red and have a sweeter flavor.

SQUASH, SUMMER: Don't let these get much longer than 6 to 8 inches. Large squash have tough skin and fibrous flesh.

SQUASH, WINTER: These are ready when the skins have toughened. When pressed with a thumbnail, they shouldn't puncture.

STRAWBERRIES: A ripe berry has no traces of green and is nice and plump. Pick with the caps on.

SWISS CHARD: Cut a few outer leaves from each plant as needed, as soon as they reach usable size (4 to 6 inches for tender greens, larger for stuffing). Keep harvesting all season long.

TOMATOES: The red color is a dead giveaway of a ripe tomato. Pick before they start to soften.

Storage Requirements of Vegetables and Fruits

Cold and Very Moist
(32°–40°F; 90–95% relative humidity)

Beets
Broccoli (short term)
Brussels sprouts (short term)
Carrots
Celery
Chinese cabbage
Collards
Leeks
Parsnips
Rutabagas
Turnips

Cool and Moist
(40°–50°F; 85–90% relative humidity)

Cucumbers
Eggplants (50°–60°F)
Muskmelons (cantaloupes)
Peppers, sweet (45°–55°F)
Tomatoes, ripe
Watermelons

Cold and Moist
(32°–40°F; 80–90% relative humidity)

Apples
Cabbage
Cauliflower (short term)
Grapefruit
Grapes (40°F)
Oranges
Pears
Potatoes
Quinces

Cool and Dry
(35°–40°F; 60–70% relative humidity)

Garlic
Onions
Soybeans, green, in the pod (short term)

Moderately Warm and Dry
(50°–60°F; 60–70% relative humidity)

Peppers, hot (dried)
Pumpkins
Squash, winter
Sweet potatoes
Tomatoes, green (tolerate up to 70°F)

PANTRY RECORDS

ITEM	HOW MUCH	STOCKING-UP METHOD	NOTES

Pantry Records

Item	How Much	Stocking-Up Method	Notes

PLANS FOR NEXT SEASON'S GARDEN

USDA Plant Hardiness Zone Map

The USDA Plant Hardiness Zone Map was developed by the USDA's Agricultural Research Service to help growers determine which plants are best suited for their particular region.

Looking on the map, you'll see that the United States and southern Canada are divided into climatic zones based on the average annual minimum temperature of each region. The colder the zone, the lower the number. To discover the zone you live in, simply find your location on the map and read the key for the appropriate shaded area.

When you're buying plants, consult catalogs and books to find out which hardiness zone the plants will do well in. If you're in Zone 7 and you see a plant that is recommended for Zones 5–9 or labeled "Hardy to Zone 6," you can expect the plant to do well in your area. If you live in Zone 3, you'll need to select a more cold-tolerant plant.

Keep in mind there are climatic variations within each region—and even within each garden. Your garden's immediate climate may be different from that of your region overall. Many factors—including altitude, wind exposure, proximity to bodies of water, terrain, and shade—can cause variations in growing conditions by as much as two zones in either direction.

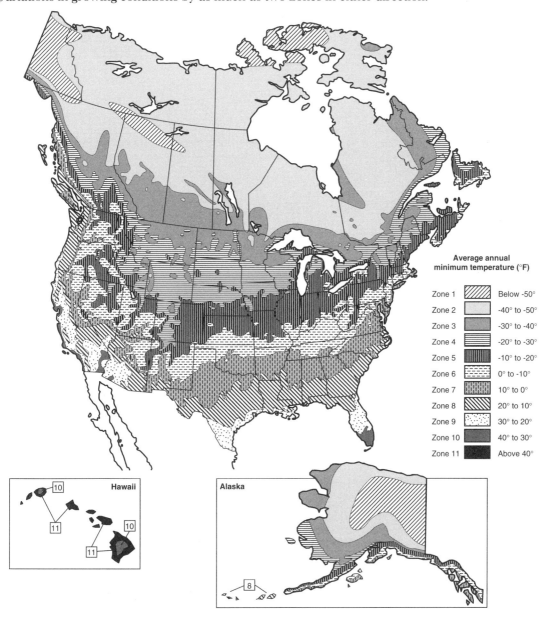

Average annual minimum temperature (°F)

Zone 1		Below -50°
Zone 2		-40° to -50°
Zone 3		-30° to -40°
Zone 4		-20° to -30°
Zone 5		-10° to -20°
Zone 6		0° to -10°
Zone 7		10° to 0°
Zone 8		20° to 10°
Zone 9		30° to 20°
Zone 10		40° to 30°
Zone 11		Above 40°

Hawaii

Alaska

GARDENING SOURCES

Here's a handy place to jot down addresses, phone numbers, and more for sources offering gardening supplies, plants, seeds, courses, and information.

NAME AND ADDRESS	PHONE, FAX, E-MAIL, AND WEBSITE	COMMENTS

Name and Address	Phone, Fax, E-mail, and Website	Comments

YEAR IN REVIEW

This calendar is useful for long-range plans. Write down appointments, birthdays, anniversaries, gardening tasks and other dates so you can quickly check what's coming up in the next few weeks.

MONTH	SUNDAY	MONDAY	TUESDAY	WEDNESDAY	THURSDAY	FRIDAY	SATURDAY
January						1	2
	3	4	5	6	7	8	9
	10	11	12	13	14	15	16
	17	18	19	20	21	22	23
	24	25	26	27	28	29	30
	31						
February		1	2	3	4	5	6
	7	8	9	10	11	12	13
	14	15	16	17	18	19	20
	21	22	23	24	25	26	27
	28						
March		1	2	3	4	5	6
	7	8	9	10	11	12	13
	14	15	16	17	18	19	20
	21	22	23	24	25	26	27
	28	29	30	31			
April					1	2	3
	4	5	6	7	8	9	10
	11	12	13	14	15	16	17
	18	19	20	21	22	23	24
	25	26	27	28	29	30	
May							1
	2	3	4	5	6	7	8
	9	10	11	12	13	14	15
	16	17	18	19	20	21	22
	23	24	25	26	27	28	29
	30	31					
June			1	2	3	4	5
	6	7	8	9	10	11	12
	13	14	15	16	17	18	19
	20	21	22	23	24	25	26
	27	28	29	30			